18 MONEY ENERGY LAWS

VALENTINA WHITE

INSPIRED WORLD PUBLISHING

ACKNOWLEDGMENTS

1. Kristina Masiuliene - Transcriber

2. Linda Bucksey - Book cover designer and artist for all of the illustrations found in this book.

CONTENTS

Gratitude.

I am grateful to God for the divine power guiding me in my way and for material abundance manifesting in spiritual wealth. God and I are one. God is always flourishing. And this is why I am flourishing as well.

I constantly am in vibrations of the highest intelligence. All my achievements rely on truth.

Let it be so at all levels. In all realities. Here and now. For me and those around me.

Foreword by Milda Sabiene

Everyone can be wealthy! And the relationship with money starts with the wallet! Seriously? Absolutely!!!

We each have a unique relationship with money and its energy. But I'm sure we all want to live in abundance because we can only share when we have something to share.

Working in finance and working with money every day, Valentina put the basic all money energy laws into one amazing book. Both the beginner and already advanced will find the answers to the questions that concern them.

The book is laid out and written simply and clearly. It describes in a structured way the main financial principles that lead to abundance. Valentina shares simple and effective solutions that the reader can implement in practice.

You will gain so much from this book, so sit back, relax and learn about the 18 Money Energy Laws.

~ Milda Sabiene, holistic coach, business psychologist and 3 x international bestselling author

THE BEGINNING

I was born in Mazeikiai, a small town in Samogitia, Lithuania. I lived in Druskininkai as a child, then moved to Kelme, Vilnius, and Kaunas. I have had 23 places of residence, thus learning to adapt, make friends, and fit in with life all over again. My parents were ordinary people: my dad was a jack-of-all-trades, who did whatever he set out to do, and my mum was a trader, a clever woman, who was able to feed us three children, cooking, baking and stewing whatever she could afford to buy after our parents got divorced. As far as I remember, our family was always short of money—we had the bare necessities, and luxuries just did not exist. There were no successful people around me that I could look up to—no inspirational leaders. Life was very simple, and the plan was also clear (as it is for most people): school, university, work, retirement, death. I followed this plan to move forward. After graduating from high school, I went to university and got a job. I would get up, go to work, earn a living, eat, and go to bed. Doing the same thing the next day—many days were the same. I always had a feeling that something was missing in this life. Inside, I resisted the stagnation, the false security of having a permanent job—that boring, restrictive life plan. I wanted more and in a different way. I have always felt different and liked to do things differently. I was a nerd, and others saying "you are so weird" felt like the best compliment.

I first realised that money is more than just paper quite early on—at the age of 22. I lived in a small rented room at the time, which barely fit a sofa bed, a small wardrobe, and a desk. I was a full-time student, working as a waitress in a bar after lectures. I was in lectures from 9 am to 4 pm and from 5 pm to 7 am, I was at work. I was used to sleeping a few hours a day, dozing off in the first lectures at the university. I used to spend all my money on living, always running out of money. One day, I ran out of money, with three weeks still remaining until payday. Although the lack of money was nothing new, and I was trying to manage as best I could, I was in a panic. I felt that I had various emotional/psychological ailments—I wanted to heal them without the intervention of traditional medicine by delving deeper into the causes and origins of the disorders. I looked for sources that would give at least some answers. That's how I came into possession of **J. Murphy's** book "**The Power of Your Subconscious Mind**". This is the book I was reading at that time, which was most difficult both financially and emotionally. It is a book about the ability of a human being to subconsciously, by working on oneself, to heal, and to create whatever life you want. It was a completely new and unexpected idea for me back then. Even though I panicked inside and wanted to find comfort in someone, to ask for money, my cat-like curiosity encouraged me to investigate the power of the subconscious mind as described in the book —I started to transform the negative intrusive thoughts about money that kept coming: "How to survive for another three weeks? How will I pay to get to work? How will I buy food?" I wanted to try thought transformation, so I played a game—I imagined I had money, leading myself to the state of peace of mind. After working on myself for a few hours, I started to believe that everything was happening for my own good and that I could be absolutely calm, trusting the universe to take care of me in some way. I retained that calm state of mind. I still remember it as if it was today: two days later, on Saturday morning, I heard the doorbell ring. I opened the door and saw my ex-boyfriend, who I broke up with six months ago, standing there. Of course, I was surprised and asked him what he was doing here. He said: "Hi there, here you are," and stretched out his hand to give me money. Then adding: "I don't know why, but I thought you may need it now." I remember taking the money with surprise and joy. Surprised by what trust in the universe can do and joyful about the practice having worked in such an incredible way. Later in my life, I have forgotten this power, going through ups and downs, experiences and lessons—I have changed jobs, I have had various addictions, and I have been in toxic relationships. I thank the universe that my painful experiences and inexhaustible perseverance have become an incentive to search for a different life—more meaningful and richer both spiritually and materially—life in abundance, which I have dreamt of.

In 2010, I emigrated to the United Kingdom, to England. At that time in Lithuania, I felt there were limits to my potential. No, I didn't know what I wanted. It was only my inner voice that screamed that I wanted something more, so I dove into wider waters without a clear plan, without really knowing what I was going to do.

In 2013, I founded a finance company in London. I took this step with absolutely no business experience, but with a burning desire to have my own business and to do quality work—to empower a vocation I was still discovering. Money has become a powerful tool in my life. I have advised more than 7,000 people on a wide range of accounting and financial issues, with consultations lasting from 5 minutes to 5 hours. I met all kinds of people. *The biggest lesson I learnt is **that everyone has money!*** But not everyone knows what to do with it. I also had to tame money. That's when I started earning money and felt the power of luxury—I spent money quickly and in large sums. I wanted to have everything—fancy dresses, leather shoes, a new car, etc. I ate at expensive restaurants and got into debt—I didn't understand the energy laws of money back then. My personal credit cards and loans amounted to £60,000. My business was also in debt (around £50,000)—after all, I started it from a loss, not a zero. Today, I stand straight and proud of myself because by taking the time to understand and empower the Money Energy Laws (which was hard work on myself over a number of years), I paid off all my debts in nine months!

When my financial situation got better or worse (constant unpredictable jumps, both when I changed jobs and when I started my own company), I kept asking myself: "Why is that? Why do other people live stable lives and never run out of money while I am always borrowing? Why is it that my money leaves easily and never comes back, while others get all of it and more, like an inexhaustible resource? Why, after getting a flow of money, do I lose it? Why do I earn a lot and still have no money?" I used to marvel at how people around me were able to spend their money happily and not worry about tomorrow. At the same time, I would come back after shopping with just a few clothes and shoes and instantly feel the emptiness and anxiety of lost finances inside. I was trying to find the answers, and I was determined to learn, to experience things first-hand, so I did the simplest and silliest practices, like putting my wallet in order.

I got a training session with a prominent Russian millionaire oligarch who has 37 sources of income—I was looking forward to them like a miracle. I was hoping for a special recipe that would open the path to riches. All I got was an unexpected and simple piece of advice: "Get your wallet in order." I was expecting tough assignments, but he told me to get my wallet in order. I laughed heartily and started to doubt the teacher's competence, even resisting: "How can my wallet affect my financial situation?" But my curiosity and determination were once again a little stronger than my old programmes. I got my wallet in order. Because, according to my teacher, this is where it all starts. I felt it in my finances. A wallet acts as a law of attraction.

With my wallet in order, I continued my search because I had already experienced the law of attraction—I had started to attract five times my income. But the trick was that as much money came in, so much of it went out, and gradually more came out than went in. My cash flow was high and grew steadily by 30% each year, but I still had no money. So I was looking for those other answers, especially for one powerful tool, one miracle training that would help me get my financial situation in order and always have money. And my biggest dream was to get out of debt! At the time, this dream seemed unattainable, and I thought I would live in debt for the rest of my life. I hadn't yet experienced what it was like to live in abundance because my mind was full of resistance and blocks. But I was very keen to try all the techniques indiscriminately. A little here, a little there, but with short-lived results. One teacher had one tool, another one or two tools. But I could not get a lasting result and an answer. I was ready to work hard and intensively on myself for a year or more, but I didn't know how to do it correctly and effectively—I never got that one tool that would give me a lasting, permanent result. I had to create such a tool myself. I continued to observe people, study the energy of money and try different tools myself. I used to write down all my observations until one day, I saw that I had 18 discoveries. I structured them and called them laws. Initially, I applied them to the volunteers around me—I am thankful to my relatives and clients who believed in me and accepted the tool I created to awaken abundance.

I have invested more than £150,000 in my self-education and various studies. I studied the psychology of money, attended various workshops, and had online practices with teachers. I had and still have my teachers. I am in a constant state of development and establishment of a relationship with the world. And I like it. Today, I still live in London and have my own accountancy company, which was awarded Best Finance Company in West London in 2020 and 2021. I have three businesses and seven sources of income, and I am increasing them because I accept abundance by giving value to others. I have put all my cash flow experience into a unique programme—the "18 Money Energy Laws". They may seem nothing new, they may seem familiar, but they have become the laws of a successful life for my clients and me. These laws apply and work for everyone, without exception, just like the laws of the Universe or nature. A person who has mastered all the 18 Money Energy Laws lives in constant natural abundance. Even if a person's income decreases, it has no impact on his lifestyle and comfort choices. My clients are already learning these laws privately. This tool is available in the White Growth Studio. I want to thank my clients, who helped me gain even more experience and all those who are starting their unique journey towards permanent abundance.

True happiness is a balance between spiritual fulfillment and material satisfaction.

The balance between the amount of money and being conscious is a delicate one. It is definitely not black or white.

If we want to be spiritual by giving up money, then we should think about detachment from society, devotion to the Earth, and eventually a monastic life. But life is possible in harmony with finances and consciousness-raising spiritual growth. Finances come through a conscious relationship with own self and money.

Going for great wealth + inner vanity = waste of financial energy.

Excessive spirituality + poverty = lack of financial literacy.

Whatever I do in my life, I remember the Great Balance. Whether it's a balance sheet in financial statements or a balance sheet of self-

sự hiển dâng

development, love, dedication, growth, nutrition—I am always looking for My Balance.

18 Money Energy Laws is not a seminar, lecture, or training. I believe in perseverance and consistent work that delivers results. The 18 Money Energy Laws are the inspiration of my experience, technology, and tool for opening a personal channel of abundance. And ways to use this transformation tool can be learnt. It is what you will learn, experience, and make a part of yourself.

WALLET

WALLET

W hen my journey to financial abundance began, I observed and tried it all. I learnt more about getting a wallet in order from my beloved teacher, and I took a whole course on it. I have put the theory into practice and can now confidently say that financial success starts with a wallet.

The *law of wallet* is the first law I want to describe and communicate. A wallet plays a rather important role in people's lives. It is a symbol of money, of abundance, so the law of wallet acts like a law that attracts or, conversely, repels finances. Imagine your wallet is a big magnet. It draws into itself and your environment what it contains, how it is arranged and what it is like itself. After all, it's the simplest law of attraction—my environment is what I am. And I am what my environment is. My wallet is what I am.

In this Chapter, I want to give you a piece of advice on what your wallet and its contents should look like, how to change or improve your attitude towards cash, and how to attract financial success into your life.

At the end of the chapter, I will look at the importance of a respectful and honest relationship with the environment and oneself and the importance of the choices people make that determine the natural flow of money. I want to emphasise that I am not talking about attracting an illusory million pounds/dollars, euros. I am talking about a constant flow of natural money energy—when there is always money in my life. Even if there is less, I don't feel short. This is what I propose to attract into your life, once you have sorted out all the laws of money energy—starting with the simplest thing = your wallet.

I have been working in finance for many years, meeting all kinds of people, observing them, and dealing with their financial affairs. I can safely say that everyone has money. The only difference is who uses the money, how they use it, what they do with it, and what relationships they build with it. Unfortunately, most people don't even realise that in order to constantly have money, they need to invest in building a relationship with money.

I have tested all the laws myself. I just wanted to fundamentally change my family's money karma—those constant financial ups and downs from having money to having nothing or being in debt. And I wasn't ashamed to try it all - even to the point of absurdity in the eyes of others. Once I got all the laws in order, I felt a special satisfaction in my relationship with money. An orderly wallet seemed, to me, the least logical law, but it worked, giving a clear result. That's why I am now using my knowledge and experience to advise my clients, giving them the opportunity to put the abundance of money back into their lives. I am very fond of structured texts, so I will list the principles of the law of wallet in bullet points.

1. WALLET QUALITY

First of all, a wallet itself must be *high quality and expensive.* Natural leather is preferred. I recommend investing in one because a luxury wallet is valuable in itself and helps attract cash flow into your life. A quality wallet is the first sign that a person cares about where and how his money is kept. This reveals a person's attitude towards money in general, which also determines the flow of finances in life. Having restored and maintained a good relationship with money, a person can afford a bohemian, simple, or handmade wallet.

I observe wallets of the middle and wealthy class and notice that they are expensive, often designer, wallets. These people invest in a wallet itself because they feel this law at the subconscious level. Meanwhile, wallets of the poor (and here I mean people with a poor person's mentality) tend to be cheap, worn out, or even worse, bought in a thrift shop or inherited. Living in a circle of negative money energy, they either become poorer or balance by borrowing more. As long as a person has a shabby and unorganised wallet, the level of his finances will stay the same, as if preserved. To move from the economically poor to the middle or wealthy class, changing a wallet is essential, investing in it and buying a quality one. Or, even better, ordering a personalised wallet. This is how the law of attraction of money comes into play.

About 1% of the world's population, especially the rich, do not carry wallets. They have moved on to the next financial level and have structured their lives in such a way as to avoid having to pay by cash or card all the time. This is usually the category of people who understand the value of the money they earn, appreciate it, and regulate its flow.

The visual condition of a wallet thus reflects the financial condition of its owner. This is one of the most important aspects of the law of wallet and the natural energy of money.

2. RESPECT FOR MONEY

When I say "respect for money", I mean that I treat money with the same respect as all life in the world. I respect every form of life. When I walk down the street carrying rubbish in my hand, I think: how nice it is to walk down a clean street, and I throw the rubbish into a dustbin rather than throwing it on the street. When I put goods in my shopping basket, I do it carefully, respectfully, lovingly, because I will later eat and use them. So when I put money in my wallet, I also consciously put it in order. It is therefore important to have *a straight* wallet. A lot of people, especially men, like folded wallets. Bills in a wallet must be flat, straight, and orderly. It is also very important that bills are stacked in the same way from largest to smallest. I recommend choosing a larger, straight, sturdy wallet and avoiding folding bills. As I said, men are very fond of folded wallets. Most people have such wallets and buy them out of habit, forgetting about the straight-wallet alternative and thinking about convenience. It's just like in relationships. If you live with someone who is comfortable, but there is nothing else there besides comfort: no love, no connection, no mutual benefit, so what is the point of such a relationship? To get the result out of your wallet, I recommend buying the right, rather than a comfortable, one. Let's build a beautiful relationship between you, your wallet, and your money.

If you are stubbornly going for a folded wallet, then I suggest you choose one with the gentlest possible bending angle to minimise the bending of the bills carried in it. However, I want to reemphasise that bills should be treated with the utmost respect. I have seen examples in major supermarkets of people taking a crumpled wad of cash out of their pocket and throwing it at the cashier as if he was not a human being altogether. This is an obvious case of a lack of respect for money, for the environment, and for oneself, which confirms the functioning of the law of a wallet. Such behaviour closes doors to financial opportunities and often leads to people asking themselves why they find it so difficult to manage their money. They blame politicians, parents, employers, children, friends, but not themselves. As long as this mentality towards finance prevails, we are guaranteed to spin in a field of negative money energy.

A straight wallet gives you the opportunity to keep your money neatly organised, thus showing your attitude towards it. If I treat money with respect, the energy of money will do the same—I get what I give—Law of attraction.

3. COLOUR

I recommend a purse *in red*, as it is the colour of luxury. But if you buy a wallet of a different colour, that's fine. In this case, the tip is to put, or better still, to sew in a piece of red silk in it. Silk also symbolises luxury and opulence, so carrying around this piece of material will help to attract the natural, permanent energy of money. It's like a bonus, an added value, that promotes money circulation.

4. BANK CARDS

I advise you to keep *debit bank cards only* in your wallet: no credit cards, discount cards, or vouchers. A credit card is a debt, in other words, negative energy that sucks money out. Keeping credit cards together with debit cards sets you up to be in debt all the time. If you have credit cards, they should be stored separately, either in a compartment in your handbag or in a separate small wallet for cards.

5. CASH

Always have *cash* in your wallet. I recommend always having cash bills in it, as this is how the law of attraction works: money attracts money. An empty wallet can only attract the emptiness you want to avoid. Cheques, receipts, and gift vouchers should be kept separate from money, as they add to the load and hinder the free flow of positive money energy. Receipts in your wallet = rubbish in your wallet. It is best to keep them away from your wallet. A wallet must contain cash, debit cards, a driving licence, and an identity document.

6. PRECIOUS METAL

I recommend carrying a precious metal—gold or silver—in your wallet. It must be pure—avoid gold or silver plated. Gold is a more valuable and more desirable metal with a stronger performance. Silver is a good second place choice. A gold/silver coin or a piece of gold (no matter what size) should be placed in a separate compartment in your wallet, possibly with a piece of red silk. Precious metals attract money because, from a historical perspective, money was made from gold or silver in ancient times. The rise of the global financial markets started with precious metals. And now, the value of money is linked to gold and silver. The entire market is based on the fluctuation of these metals. Investing in gold and silver is one way to preserve your wealth. Gold also has the ability to multiply income. I'll talk about this in another chapter.

Gold coins are a symbol of abundance, so I advise you to carry them in your wallet and observe how the law of attraction works.

7. INHERITING MONEY ENERGY

Inheriting a wallet from your parents, other owners, or **buying a second-hand one is a really bad idea**—the wallet of another person = the energy of another. Each person develops own relationship with money and energy field. Therefore, the financial energy of the owner of the wallet is transferred with the wallet. Let's say a person has lived by borrowing and taking over his wallet, I also get some of the financial energy he has accumulated, which is dragged like a train into my life, and the failures recur. I encode myself with the money energy of another person and live in a vicious circle. That's why having your own wallet is very important.

For example, my close acquaintance, who is naturally talented, intelligent, and active, is constantly facing financial problems—not being paid, being cheated, or being robbed. He is in constant financial downs and deprivation. Of course, he has serious unresolved issues related to all the laws of monetary energy. But first of all, he has his father's wallet. His father was barely making ends meet and had a hard time making a living. Some of his father's karma has been taken over with the wallet, leading to my acquaintance's natural money energy going backwards. The other seventeen laws of money energy in his life have not been organized either, but the inherited wallet immediately caught my eye and answered the question of why it is so difficult for him to get his life in order on the financial level.

A quality, luxurious and clean wallet that always has a piece of gold/silver and a piece of red silk, orderly arranged money (it has to be bills—cash), debit cards, no extra junk in it, and one that circulates a positive money energy, is bound to attract potential and favourable situations that will bring financial rewards into your life. The law of wallet works effectively. But empowering it is important, attracting natural personal abundance into your life.

I have tried and experienced all the above principles of the law of a wallet myself. As long as I carried credit cards in my wallet, as long as it lacked harmony and basic order, I lived by borrowing. Here I want to note that where there is order, there also is abundance. I loved luxurious life, which I ensured for myself from a credit account. Thus I fell into debt, into a vicious cycle of negative energy. Once I got my wallet in order, I started to make a plan in my head on how to get out of debt. I imagined in my mind what life without debt looks like. I sent questions to the Universe and received answers in the form of signs, situations, and opportunities. I noticed that I found new ways to earn money and that my life was filled with favourable circumstances and people. I started to build a relationship with money and to empower positive money energy. But I want to emphasise that once you get your wallet in order, don't expect a sudden miracle. Remember that the miracle is you. Just follow the signs from the Universe, have patience, start acting purposefully, be respectful with your money, and financial matters will slowly start to improve. A wallet is a working law of attraction. Money that comes to your life reflects the wallet you have.

When I talk about respect for money, I want to emphasise the importance of respect in general, especially for oneself. This is an overlooked but very important aspect of the laws of attraction and the vibrations that affect them. In Latin, *respect* means *attention*. How much attention do I pay to myself and my environment? A modern human being, living in abundance and having plentiful choices, has forgotten the concept of respect. We lack respect for nature, for our neighbours, and even for ourselves. Many people lack self-confidence and view their environment through a prism of criticism, anger, and frustration. Their psychological condition often is very poor. They live in conflict with others, behaving irresponsibly—polluting the environment, driving risky, and constantly blaming others for their troubles. People with low self-esteem hurt themselves by overeating in fast food restaurants or otherwise harming their bodies—without staying fit, having no regimen or goals. That's why it's so important to develop self-respect—awareness of oneself and others. **Self-respect starts with our relationship with our environment.** If I don't respect another person, he will never come to me because I treat him badly. This is also how money energy works. After all, both people and money are energy, a vibration. **Everything is a vibration.** If I don't respect the way money is made, the money itself, I won't have it. If I value and respect another person, whatever their background, behaviour, or personality is, I still respect them, and this way, I also develop respect for myself. Such a relationship raises self-confidence and adequacy in a person. **A person becomes psychologically stable, and the end result is abundance.** When I respect others, I become a person worthy of respect. Therefore, respect for money requires respect for the environment and, in particular, *respect for oneself.* Here are some tips on how to do this.

1. To develop self-respect, you first need to be open and honest with yourself and other people. It means telling the truth. It means being a non-superficial human being and being able to live from the bottom of the heart.

2. Continually invest in self-education. Here I do not mean universities, but rather learning and gaining knowledge in any field and throughout life. Keep learning. Especially appreciating the communication and lessons of people who have experience, have seen successes and failures first-hand, and draw on the wisdom of others. Understanding the theory is a good thing, but learning from practitioners is of great value. This means that "I know" means nothing without putting knowledge into practice.

3. Understand the importance of exercise. Exercise for at least 20 minutes every day to keep fit because the body is like water—when it stands still, it starts to stink. And if the body is stagnant, the mind is also stagnant. Good physical well-being promotes activity and positive thinking.

4. Watch what you put in your mouth. Plan your diet carefully. Take time to fast and cleanse your body. Eat food that is nutritious, healthy, and shows respect for your body. Aim for a light, active body that serves and fosters a love for your own self.

5. Know your financial responsibilities. Plan your cash flow. Take responsibility for your debts—find the best way to repay them without going bankrupt.

6. Learn to listen to other people regardless of what their experience is, whether you like it or not. Hear them. If I can find the strength and tolerance to hear another person, I will also hear myself. I will become worthy of respect myself.

7. Foster your values. Practise good manners with yourself and others. It is important to understand who I am, what I broadcast to the world, and what my mission is.

8. Take responsibility for your behaviour. Whatever happens, the first thing to do is to turn back to my own self—what I did in a particular situation. I don't blame others, I decide what I could have done differently to get a better result. Managing to refrain from attacking others and taking responsibility automatically earns the respect of others.

9. Being able to apologise. Usually, people are always forgiving someone, for example, their parents. Try simply apologising to them. It is a very powerful and demanding practice when a person drops his

ego, swallows his pride, and perceives that he is the creator of his own being. The practice of apology opens up possibilities and provides peace, reconciliation, and a stronger sense of self-esteem.

10. **Choose your friends properly and create an attractive, mutually beneficial environment for yourself.** Notice which people are pumping out energy, which ones are motivating and sharing experiences. Mutual benefit must dominate in relationships with people. There must be an exchange of energies—I give value to another person, and he gives value to me. This bond builds strong and healthy relationships. We need to cleanse our environment of people who create negative influences and are only able to take. Let toxic people out of your environment. One must have limits if one is a giver because takers have no limits. They take as much as a giver gives. Cleaning up your contacts in social networks and in your immediate environment will make your life brighter and help you deal with other areas easier, including finances.

11. **Have your own goals and know the strategies to achieve them.** What is the purpose of life, and what are my smaller goals? What is the essence of my existence? What is the mission of my soul? Understanding this is very important.

Following these basic steps helps to develop self-respect. One day you will notice harmony and order settling in your life and relationships with people, and money changing. A clean approach to money will definitely bring your wallet in order. Harmony and respect enable a natural flow of money, allowing us to live in prosperity and meet our needs.

I want to conclude this chapter by stressing that choices are everywhere in life. If a person chooses to behave brutally, to put oneself above others, lacks respect for others and oneself, the environment will respond in the same way. If one chooses to fold money and treat it as irrelevant—to carry it in his pockets, etc.—he will get the same in return. It's a simple principle that applies everywhere. If one chooses order and abundance, puts effort into it, shows responsibility for actions and choices, including a choice of a wallet, the natural flow of money is enabled.

SENSE OF PLEASURE

2

PLEASURE

E njoying life is directly linked to personal happiness, thus to achieve more happiness, it is necessary to relearn what gives pleasure and how deep it can be felt. Google Dictionary defines pleasure as "a feeling of happy contentment and enjoyment." It is a life feeling enjoyment.

One type of pleasure is sensation. This is usually expressed through physical sensations, such as a pleasure of eating or sexual sensations. My favourite expression of pleasure is pleasure through intention—I have the intention and the will to feel pleasure, and I create it myself. I also feel this pleasure spending money. This is the essence of the second law—the law of pleasure.

In the past, I used to spend money with fear that there is and will be no money, with self-criticism that I shouldn't let myself buy a good thing, with anxiety that I did not know how I would live if I lost a certain amount. Only when I started pursuing changes and observing the environment did I see that people who spend money with pleasure somehow always get back what they spend. So I started to educate, train and reprogram myself to feel plea-sure when spending money.

My personal story of the law of pleasure was really interesting. At first, I used to carefully observe rich people coming to a store and easily paying several thousand pounds for their purchases without a look of anxiety on their faces. I would think to myself: "Are they that calm after they return home? Don't they give any thought as to how they will live later? Do they still have money?" I used to consider people who shopped in designer stores as fools: "Who can buy such tasteless things for crazy money?" or "What's the point of spending £200 on a sweater when I can buy one for £20?". One thing I've noticed all the people who spent large sums of money in common was them spending it with pleasure, without any resistance. I decided that I needed to work on this and start enjoying shopping at more expensive stores. And after extensive work on myself, I realised why it's worth happily paying £200 or even £500 for a cashmere sweater:

• because it's warm, comfortable, and soft,

• because it looks much better on me than a cheaper one,

• because I wear it longer and with more pleasure,

• because it does not lose its shape several or several dozen times longer than a cheap one,

• because I appreciate quality,

• because I know that I am worth wearing it.

Now I even get pleasure from paying my utilities!

The law of pleasure is a powerful force in all areas and throughout life: at home, at work, and in free time. It is very important to do things consciously, with the intention to feel pleasure and enjoy the moment of being. Seek satisfaction in absolutely all circumstances, even when bad things happen. *If things didn't work out the way I wanted, this means they worked out the way that was good for me.* It is a powerful healing thought. Understand and accept that everything is for my own good. It's important to trust a situation that teaches me something, that gives me experience, even if I can't see it right away. Feel a complete satisfaction with own life: relationships, home, work environment—the satisfaction of doing administrative work, looking after a pet, preparing for a trip, cooking lunch. In principle, it's about the pleasure of living and the pursuit of satisfaction.

The law of pleasure is also closely linked to money. Once you have developed the ability to consciously spend money with pleasure, the law of multiplication of money opens up. I will tell you how it works. Most people have a *saver's* mentality—pinching every penny. Although, in fact, they earn enough to afford one or another thing, or some entertainment. These people look for special offers, and their decision to buy depends on the price (usually low). You can look at the price, and weighing the value for money is absolutely necessary, but avoid the principle "I only buy when it's cheap," which is often misleading, resulting in making unnecessary purchases. All things around you should evoke a positive emotion. Otherwise, there is no point in having them. That's why you should buy with pleasure. Let's say I go to a shop, touch a cashmere dress, and feel the pleasure I will feel wearing it, how it will fit me and feel good on my body. I already have pleasant feelings just imagining wearing this dress. And I buy it with the greatest pleasure. I prefer quality over price. I notice women who have the fostered archetype of the Queen! They always choose quality products or services only. Such women choose to have less, but better quality. Such behaviour transmits the perception that I am worth spending money on myself. I earn. I consciously allow myself to buy something that will make me happy. I am not talking about, say, the psychotic shopping on Black Friday, when people buy in a hurry, a lot, and with imaginary discounts. It is a crazy mass buying that lacks awareness. Black Friday discounts are not big. The same discounts are also available at Christmas and sales. By being conscious, I avoid the feeling of acting like sheeple and buy responsibly and with pleasure.

A study conducted in 136 countries around the world found that people who are more likely to spend their money are happier than those who are reluctant spenders. Another study showed that people are even happier when they spend money on others instead of themselves. Another law of money energy in action = charity.

I want to emphasise the importance of spending money on your own needs as a way of showing love for yourself. If I want a new sweater, I go and buy it. Not just some random sweater, but the one that brings positive emotions in me, feels good on my body, and has a clear purpose. People are full of all sorts of social clichés and imposed beliefs that all they have is their last money. That is the biggest lie. They limit themselves, and limitations strengthen their blocks. Traumas and blocks take people away from the natural flow of life, and they live hectically, going with the flow. When there is "no" money, and you want to blame it on your employer because he doesn't appreciate you, on your husband because he doesn't behave the way you want him to, or on your spendthrift wife because your life is "miserable", point to yourself first. Because, let me repeat this once again, I am a reflection of how I treat others, myself, and money.

I am = what my environment is.

I am = what the person I love is.

I am = what my relationship with money is.

I am the only one who can change myself to have my relationship with money energy change. I keep reminding myself that my dreams are a reality. I wish to live my life—being myself, in freedom and flow. My path to this has been one of discovery and exploration, especially in the financial field, where I had many blocks. So I will tell you about my experience developing the skill of spending money with pleasure.

I used to buy clothes at Primark or similar stores—as cheap as possible, catching sales. I often bought rubbish. For example, jeans for £190 seemed like nonsense to me. I used to avoid buying good quality, more expensive clothes. Eventually, I started thinking about how I could change my buying habit and start buying with pleasure and only what I really like. I started with the basics—going to luxury stores. Actually, I didn't start with the most luxurious ones at first. This was a huge challenge for a girl from the countryside. I had to cross the threshold of fear and dare to stay in a luxury store. I say stay because I would go in the store and leave shortly afterwards with my eyes bulging with fear. I was full of a sense of *whatamIdoinghere* because I underestimated myself. I felt very bad—like a country girl thrown into a strange environment with millionaires. Then I started going to the most expensive stores. I would still look around window displays and clothes in stores which I thought to be extremely expensive. In the beginning, I didn't even see good clothes—just bits of material at very high prices. Who can pay that much? Then I started training myself—once I wanted to run outside, I would make myself stay and keep looking around. Eventually, I started touching the materials, exploring the styles—I wanted to feel the garment. I realised that there was something good in it. I started talking to sales assistants, asking them what would suit my figure, what they could recommend for one occasion or another. It was a real workout! I felt the result. I started trying on clothes—both the ones I liked and those that I didn't. I must admit, I didn't have a taste for dressing up. I searched and researched. I realised what suits me better and why expensive clothes cost a lot—they are made wisely, with quality materials, extensive labour, and knowledge. I especially felt the difference in the way the garment fit on my body.

I remember one day walking into the Shoreditch area in London filled with different stores selling quality apparel. By then, I had already developed an understanding and appreciation for quality clothes, and I already knew what I liked and what fit me. I saw some clothes that I really wanted to buy. I had £1,000 in my account. I ended up leaving the stores having spent £800 and purchased a few clothing items I really wanted but was left with £200 to live on for another three weeks. That was my turning point when I allowed myself to buy what I wanted and appreciated. I felt pleasure in imagining how I would wear those smooth materials, how uplifted and comfortable I would feel. I realised how good it feels to be able to afford to buy it. I knew I was worth it. After a few days, I received an order for £830 at work—the same amount I spent on my clothes. This is exactly how the law of pleasure works—when you spend money with satisfaction, it comes back. *Money spent consciously and with pleasure always comes back.* When I buy with the sincere intention that I am worth it, that I am happy to afford it, money circulates. The energy of money has a strong vibration and wants to come back over and over again.

The important thing is that the law of pleasure attracts money—I get back what I spend. Money has to circulate—it cannot stagnate. It's like flowing water—constant movement, change. I take pleasure in buying things, I take pleasure in donating to charity, I take pleasure in paying taxes, I take pleasure in having fun—spending and getting back—because I earn money and can afford it. I don't save because I realise that money saved for no reason "stops". The more pleasure I take, the fewer blocks I have, the more I activate the flow of money. The sooner stereotypes dissolve, the more opportunities for abundance come around. When a person suppresses the flow of money, even though he earns enough, the energy of money stops—he has to keep working hard to earn it. Once again, I want to emphasise that I am talking about the natural flow of money energy—when I have money all the time. I avoid financial spikes, and if I want to earn more, I take the opportunities and earn what I want. This is how the law of pleasure works.

Another lesson: *nothing is expensive*. I can either afford it at the moment, or I can't—no need to berate those whose services cost more than I can afford. Everyone has their own value, and everyone can choose. If I don't like it and it doesn't work for me, I leave it alone. I admire how others manage to live, and I take pleasure in learning from them if I want to. After all, nobody goes into a Porche showroom and says: "Oh, you, expensive crooks/scammers." We come and admire the beautiful cars with respect. So let's admire other people's services too. And once it becomes a habit, the results will be visible and tangible.

When I appreciate others, others start appreciating me.

Everything is a mirror.

Everything goes around.

Everything = energy.

Everything = vibration.

Everything = God (the Source).

THE POWER OF
THOUGHTS AND WORDS

3

THOUGHTS AND BELIEFS

THOUGHTS

This law states the basic principle - things that I think, say and do MUST MATCH. *I think—I say—I do.* If at least one of these does not match, we end up in an inner chaos when pursuing order, and harmony becomes difficult. Works we do no longer correspond to our aims, leading to plans falling apart and goals slipping away. We live randomly, thus getting *random* results. If I am a person who thinks one thing and does another, life is difficult for me and for those around me. I am no longer confident in what I do, losing my confidence and self-esteem. Meanwhile, those around me find it difficult to build relationships, do business, and plan their leisure time with me.

It all starts with my thoughts.

If you want to change, the *first thing you need to do is to clear out the garbage of your thoughts.* Thoughts shape a person's environment, so it is very important to understand this and to master the transformation of own thoughts from negative to positive. It's not about changing those around you, it's about changing yourself. My attitude to myself and behaviour with my own self will improve when I change my thoughts. The balance between thoughts and actions will have a positive result because taking responsibility for my thoughts, words, and actions will control and transform my being.

Note that negative thoughts are 25 times stronger than positive ones. What does this mean? Well, this means that to empower positive thoughts, more effort is needed to intensify the flow of positive thoughts —25 times more positive thinking—and only then the desired result will come. People often say they think positively but don't see any change. But no change will occur unless there is a constant transformation of thoughts from negative to positive ones. It is not enough to speak positively, say, I speak well of you, even though I curse you inside. Such "positive" thinking does not work. I have to believe in what I say fundamentally and constantly monitor my thoughts and the words and actions that accompany them. Self-monitoring and self-control is the first step towards change. This requires daily, ongoing work until it becomes a new habit.

I have seen transformations myself and have personally experienced many miraculous changes in relationships with money, business partners, and even loved ones. For example, my relationship with my brother has been quite cold for many years. It seemed like we had no connection; we were distant. When I reprogrammed my thoughts and behaviour, my relationship with him began to change—we renewed our strong connection. That connection has always been there between us, but I have created barriers through negative thinking and through the words I have spoken, which have been difficult for both of us to cross. I have regained what I could have lost for life—the connection with my loved one. I thank my empowering positive thoughts for that.

It's important to pay attention to how you communicate with your family and those around you. The words spoken to your family members and your behaviour towards them are very important. All of this shapes a mutual relationship. To test your level of awareness, you only need to spend at least one day with your family. You will immediately see where you still need to work on yourself—on your thoughts, words, and intentions.

To make the actions reflect the words, I first treat the root = thoughts.

How to train to do that? Yes, it is a real constant workout! When you catch a negative thought or a word slipping out, you immediately reprogramme it and speak out a positive phrase. For example, I just said that I have no money, I noticed that, and I immediately changed that thought in my head: "It's good to have money to meet my needs all the time." And then I say out loud: "I will refuse this time, but will accept your offer next time." You have to feel that the phrase has settled in your head and has become an everyday truth. This practice must be done on a regular basis, and the transformation of thoughts from negative to positive ones must become a habit. This must be done sincerely. Without sincere intensity, the work will bear less fruit. The result will depend on the work and efforts put in it.

Financial success is shaped in the same way—by controlling your thoughts and encouraging abundance. These days, many people have heard of affirmations—phrases that are repeated over and over for a certain number of days. The practice of affirmations is effective and produces positive results. It is the same power of thought—when often repeated, it grows stronger. It is important to understand that it is possible to have what you want and as much as you want. Money is infinite. You can print as much of it as you need. Remember that abundance comes through money, through free services, sincere help, and gifts. Once you understand it, new opportunities for money energy will open up. Your eyes will open up, and you will start seeing all the signs.

I suggest you do an experiment—take a notebook and actively observe for a week what thoughts about money come to your mind, what you say to others about money, and what phrases dominate as you speak about it. Right everything down. Is it 100% negative? How negative is it? Analyse your thoughts and words. You will be surprised at how many thoughts about money—both good and bad—you actually have. This experiment will allow you to go deeper and take more control of your stream of thoughts because people still have many beliefs and fears that pollute their minds with negative thoughts. The general cleansing of thoughts works by reprogramming:

- I have no money = I have increasingly more money;

- Earning money is hard = money comes to me in the easiest, simplest and best way;

- 1 million is a large, unattainable sum = I know exactly how I would spend 1 million;

- IF = WHEN!!!;

- BUT = AND;

- Money is hard to get = I believe I can live in abundance doing the things I love;

- I will never have money = I am grateful to live in abundance;

- It's very hard to have money = all roads to wealth are open to me;

- I have to work a lot and hard to earn money = the harder I work, the more I earn;

- I wouldn't know what to do with a large amount of money = I have all the money I want to have.

I recommend you consciously monitor your thoughts and words—what you say to others—and, having noticed some negative attitudes and words, reprogram them right here and now. Practicing in this way allows you to clear out negative thoughts and words. Once this becomes a habit, a whole different level of opportunities and people will come into your life. Positive thoughts lead to words of stronger vibrations, which attract stronger processes and results. Positive thoughts and words promote balance and abundance, the sun shines brighter, and the grass is greener.

I want to point out that there are a lot of people in the world who are rich financially but poor in their values and inside. Going for great riches with inner vanity is a waste of financial energy. Such people face a constant recurrence of major failures, deceptions, and setbacks. My teaching is based on the humility to awaken the natural flow of the energy of money, when money is always available and when abundance is always present. When a person is in the flow. In his own flow. Then he is in a high vibration, and his thinking is strong. He makes financial abundance a reality in his life through his thoughts and words. This becomes the truth of his life. It is important that thoughts and words come from within, with faith, that they coincide, and that equivalent actions accompany them. It's important to pay attention to your thoughts and words when building relationships, your environment, or creating your financial story. How I think is how I live. Thoughts and words shape life. In the same way, I get the money that I expect to earn. To change my financial situation, I first change my mind.

However, when advising clients, I often hear them say: "What is the money for anyways? I don't need it." Or: "I seek to turn away from material life and achieve spiritual enlightenment only." Those who shout loudly that they do not need money are the ones who need it most. Such people have grown up in a difficult environment (deprivation or strict control) and have been programmed to stay away from money. The combination of excessive spirituality and poverty is a simple lack of financial literacy. Those, who only pursue the spiritual world in their daily lives, have digressed from the nature of the energy of money. The energy of money is very strong and comes from the energy of love. Most people are definitely unable to handle it because this requires preparation. To be able to be friends with the energy of money, entering the energy of love is necessary. My teaching is based on all these important laws of money energy.

Enjoy your financial success and be open to money because it is open to you!

Here are some more tips on how to get closer to financial abundance:

- Interact with enterprising, curious people full of ideas. They see more opportunities, and they have strategies. They absorb their experience, grow with them, and give them their return.

- Constantly strive for results. Not for a week, not for a month, but constantly. Consistency and perseverance deliver long-term results.

- Choose the right intention—seeking to make money at any price can be disappointing. Engage in activities you love, adding value to others, and the environment will render both emotional and financial returns.

- Have a role model or mentor. Watch him and keep in contact, if possible. The right mentor becomes a guide and a great help on the path of transformation.

- You can change your life at any time—there is no age limit. The 40-50-year mark is even believed to be the perfect time for transforming one's being and taking up new activities. In other words, for living a full-fledged life, for blossoming. For some, the planets have given self-fulfilment from the age of 40-50 in particular.

- Enjoy spending money consciously. Doing it with pleasure is one of the simplest steps to help the money flow easier.

- Change negative thought patterns, unblock belief systems, and start enjoying money.

- Stop making excuses for not having money and start looking for answers with an open heart.

- Change your financial imprint, the financial story that was written by someone back in your childhood, which you still live in. Change your negative beliefs.

BELIEFS

Beliefs are formed since childhood:

• they have been passed on by parents raising us,

• they come from the environment where we interact,

• they are shaped by experiences at school, sometimes painful and disappointing,

• they come from the "picture" painted by the media—TV and the press.

Beliefs form when a certain statement is accepted as the truth and the norm and when you start subconsciously believing it. In other words, a constant stream of thoughts on the same subject forms a belief. We become what we put into ourselves. We live what we become. Beliefs are the basis for the formation of a person's attitudes and philosophy of life, morals, and values. Of course, the formation starts in the head. So, if I create a belief myself, and I live in poverty, in toxic relationships, or someone else's life based on that belief, the first thing I do is turn back to myself—disarm myself, leave people alone, and start changing. I look for ways to transform my beliefs, to reprogram my life, so that I can live the way I want and so that the changes I dream of can finally happen.

For 33 years of my life, I have lived with a variety of beliefs:

• Wealth is out of my reach because I was born into such a family.

• If my parents earned for *survival*, then I am destined to do the same.

• The only way to make big money is through fraud and theft. That means I am doomed.

• I don't need to earn a lot.

• Money is evil.

• Good people don't need money.

• If I have more money, bad things will happen to me, or I will attract bad people to my environment.

• If I have more money, I will become arrogant and vain.

These were endless beliefs that I pulled out of myself one by one and worked on each of them, reprogramming them one by one. I realised that we are not so different from computers—we can program ourselves and remove viruses, just like they do. All we have to do is to use the tools, to be consistent, and finally become the captains of our own special ships that can change direction in adverse winds.

The law of conviction prevails in all life choices. *There only are such boundaries, which we define and create ourselves.* We also successfully apply boundaries on money. If you are thinking about saving for retirement, then a retirement benefit will be all you get. If you are saving for a rainy day, a rainy day will always come. But the Creator created a life of unlimited abundance. It is only a human being himself who blocks his potential for abundance by embracing limiting beliefs. Here are some of the strongest examples of abundance-limiting beliefs:

- If you want to live, you must know how to make ends meet.

- You won't make all the money.

- Be poor but fair.

- Money doesn't grow on trees.

- Better have 100 friends than 100 euros.

- Money is evil.

- Dirty money.

- Wishing for a lot, you will get little.

- Money can't buy happiness.

- Big money corrupts people.

- Why would the poor need money?

- The rich are people who climb over other people's heads.

- Good for you that you can afford it.

- You reap what you sow.

- Money earned in blood sweat.

- Money burns a hole in pockets.

- I was born into a poor family, it's my karma.

• Not everyone can live their dreams.

• Others are more talented than me.

• No one is interested in what I have to say/show.

Having such limiting beliefs, people build walls around themselves, block their potential and run away from all opportunities in life. Let's say my profession is teaching. I stamp myself as a teacher. I'm convinced that teachers usually don't earn much, so I limit myself. If I believe that I have no chance and no hope of living in abundance, the opportunities close for me. I set my own boundaries and go no further. Then I live as if I am seeing through a fog, vaguely, and when opportunities come into my life, I just don't notice them. I don't relate them to myself or simply reject them. I start working on myself, and I ask myself the question—who am I? Maybe I'm more than a teacher, maybe I am something else...? I send out a query to the Universe—who else am I? Answers can come in many forms: suggestions, acquaintances, circumstances... And one day, I, as a teacher, I am offered to do an interior design project because someone saw potential in me. Then I consider the offer, thinking to myself that this is what I have always wanted to do, but I thought it wasn't my job, that I needed to finish my studies first, or that it was impossible to make money from a hobby. It doesn't matter that I am a teacher, as I have always told myself, and I accept the opportunity. Feeling the call from within, I go and do it. This leads to other sources of income and often to the budding of activities you love. Expanding boundaries or removing blocks brings us closer to self-fulfilment and abundance. Now I realise that I am not just a profession or my job. I have many ego roles and can be whatever I want to be. It is possible. I choose to believe in myself alone, and I do it with an open heart.

Changing beliefs requires an intention and persistent work. To achieve transformation, I recommend engaging in self-development and seeking help from a professional—someone you trust, someone you feel comfortable with. It's a lot of work on oneself. This can include a variety of methods: self-monitoring and self-development, meditation, coaching sessions, hypnosis sessions, and other practices. Everyone finds the right tools, but complexity and coherence are very important here. I use these practices in courses held at the White Growth Studio. Beliefs relating specifically to money, the energy of money, are changed in the course "18 Money Energy Laws". The biggest breakthroughs for my clients come from reprogramming their beliefs and words, so I can say with confidence that it works. In general, when a person sincerely invests time working on himself, it is simply impossible not to have results. There are always results. The only difference is their extent. Some have more beliefs, and others have less. Once beliefs are sorted out and thoughts reprogrammed, a massive change takes place.

What I think and what I say are equally important. When I change my thoughts and beliefs, what I say and do changes as well—consequences correspond to what I do. The law of cause and effect prevails. The power of the subconscious mind is one of the strongest energies. The subconscious mind knows all the answers, and we can learn to get to those answers, for example, through meditation, trained intuition, and coming images or dreams. The subconscious mind glorifies change. Meanwhile, our brain is designed to keep a person in his comfort zone where everything is known and familiar. Transformation always, with no exceptions, happens when you leave your comfort zone. Give yourself permission to be successful. When releasing the permission, resistance dissolves. That energy goes upwards, returning results to the person.

Everything in life is energy rather than physical matter. *Money is also energy*. The environment is created through thoughts, words, and deeds. By mastering the flow of positive thoughts and words, beliefs are transformed, and big blocks that have been holding you back all your life are removed. Money becomes whatever you want it to be. I wish you the best of luck in fulfilling your financial desires. I emphasize YOUR desires because you should only look inside yourself—your needs, your goals—rejecting societal influences and established norms. To live the way I want, with as much money as I need. To be in complete harmony with my own self and the Universe, accepting abundance and thanking for the life I have created.

BELIEFS AND HABITS

4

HABITS

Habits shape beliefs. Beliefs shape thoughts. Thoughts shape life.

Harmful habits take people away from their natural abundance, away from their chosen path, and block opportunities. People have a lot of negative habits that complicate their life, making it difficult to plan or follow a plan, to pursue their dreams, to earn as much as they want to earn, and as much as they can earn, according to the natural energy of money that is given to them. In my practice, communication, and working with my clients, I have found that certain habits are very powerful and impede progress. I have identified 17 harmful habits that limit people's financial resources and block opportunities.

1. CONSTANT COMPLAINING

It's a habit of constantly complaining about everything and everyone. You have probably met people who see nothing but problems around them, who lack confidence, and who complain that life has been frugal to them. Their vocabulary is full of NOTs: not given, not destined, not working out, not suitable, not available... They believe that it is the environment, being "out of the cards," that causes their troubles, and they dive into the role of victim. They constantly complain to relatives, neighbours, and colleagues when they could simply try to resolve the situation. The habit of complaining drains a person's time and energy and depletes their potential. When a person focuses this energy on solving a problem, he actually manages to find solutions and the best way to solve the situation.

The habit of complaining about a lack of money must be broken. When I say I don't have money, it creates negative attitudes that lead to hardships and a constant lack of money. Words and thoughts materialise, and I continue to feel poor.

If something unplanned happens to me, something out of my way, I sit down and think: "How can I resolve this situation? What should I do?" When I formulate a question, the Universe answers it, which makes things work faster and smoother. The answer comes, sometimes faster, sometimes later, but it always comes. I have the intention to find the answer, and I repeat the question when I cook lunch, when I shop, and when I go for a walk—I keep asking: what is the best way to solve the situation?—The answer comes as signs, situations, acquaintances, and events. We need to watch the signs with an open heart. We must eradicate the habit of complaining and replace it with the habit of solving any situation. In short, we have to take responsibility.

2. WANTING HERE AND NOW

I have met many people who are excellent professionals in their field, who work for companies or large corporations; in other words, they work for someone else—they are employed. These employees have enormous potential and could quit their jobs and start their own businesses, but *they don't want to earn less*. Often, they want to get the same or even double the salary which they make in their employment right from the start of their own business. They say that they are comfortable with this attitude and want to maintain a stable income. The desire to get everything *here and now* without investing in their own future—business, income, freedom, and knowledge—is a big drag at the financial level. The expected results come from taking it slow, with consistency, building a business idea, and planning strategies with flair. Having taken big leaps, people often turn back. This is because things are done in haste, overlooking or missing something. Correcting mistakes costs a lot of human resources and often leads to an emotional pitfall and frustration. It is very important to be clear about what you want and to move in that direction in a focused, deliberate and self-paced way.

I know what I want—I figure out how to get there—I do not rush if I don't know the answer—I take small steps towards my goal—eventually, I get the answers, and I achieve the goal.

3. JEALOUSY

This harmful habit of being jealous of others often leads to gossip—gossiping about neighbours and relatives, going through their lives, counting other people's money, condemning and criticizing their actions, judging and discussing lifestyles of others. It is a waste of time and a build-up of negative energy within and around you.

There is a common stereotype that a wealthy person is a scammer, a manipulator, doing something dirty, a tax evader, etc. Thus transforming the approach to wealth is very important. Because denying money puts a strong block at the financial level. Going back to the subject of beliefs is necessary, as this is a belief—a personal truth that forms a habit; thus, I recommend reprogramming this negative belief into a statement: "A person can earn and retain wealth by being honest and open with himself and others." Jealousy is a state of very low vibrations where attracting success is impossible. Everything I vibrate out comes back to me. My habits shape my environment—my present and future. When I'm jealous, I get stuck. When I change my attitude, I start to succeed. Gossip and jealousy must be eradicated and replaced with positive energy. How can you do it? *Develop a habit of congratulating and learning from successful people.* I replace jealousy with an open congratulations/ conversation with a successful person. Let's say my neighbour lives in a luxury house, is in excellent health, has a wonderful family, and has a thriving business. I am changing the habit of being jealous of him into a habit of congratulating and rejoicing. I simply walk up to and sincerely congratulate him—I give him a handshake, a token of respect, and ask: "Listen, where is the key to your success? How do you manage to live like this? What rituals or practices do you have? What are your habits? Can you share your experience?" I am openly interested in his success. And often, I get an answer that motivates me, broadens my horizons, forms a positive habit and the environment around me, and takes me to high vibrations—the vibrations of that person.

I always congratulate, respect, learn and see opportunities.

4. SPEND MORE THAN YOU EARN

If you have a habit spending more money than earning, this path leads directly to growing debts. Inability to create a budget, unconsciously spending to quell bad moods, spending in order to show off to others, buying junk — takes to low vibrations, closing the money circle, and drowning in debt. Debt vibrations attract debt only. What to do to change this habit? First, start planning your budget and see what expenses are absolutely necessary. Second, develop the habit of paying regular attention to family/ personal budget planning. Thirdly, buy consciously—only the things you need and enjoy. This can be achieved, it's just a matter of calculating, watching yourself, and closing the debt cycle.

5. PROCRASTINATION : sự trì hoãn

It's a habit of procrastinating chores. Each person is given their flow of money energy. When a person procrastinates, his cash flow stops. Money wants to circulate, but it can't because a person's actions prevent money from coming in. "I'll do it tomorrow," "I'll do it another day, but not now"—that's self-harm. For example, I have to send out a job enquiry, but I postpone it until Monday. What happens? By procrastinating, I step in and stop the money flow.

Delay of activities, improvement of habits, self-development, sports, travel... Finally, a person wakes up at 60 and says: "After all, I didn't live the life I wanted, and now it's too late."

I replace the habit of procrastination with the habit of doing now / starting to do now. Because once I start doing, it becomes clear how to do it. Answers come from doing.

6. HAVING NO GOALS AND PLANS

Plans and goals help give meaning to life so that change can start and so that the Universe knows your desires and sends the necessary acquaintances, events, circumstances. When a person doesn't know what he wants out of life—when he doesn't have a goal, when he doesn't plan his steps for a day, a week, a year—life goes on randomly. People wonder why the laws do not work. But how can something work without any goals and a plan? Getting into the habit of planning your time/ life, visualising your goals and plans on paper or in your imagination, having short-term and long-term goals, and reviewing them regularly, brings you closer to the life you want. When the Universe gets my requests, it shows me the paths to get where I want to go.

7. CHOOSING TV OVER BOOKS AND SOCIALISING

Television is a source that captivates and absorbs time. It shapes distorted beliefs and changes habits. Much of the information broadcast on television is fake and presented to the masses as truth. Television content is created by the media, which uses various popularity tricks, stimulating strong emotions in viewers (including anger and fear as the most powerful emotions), advertising, and stereotyping. It is very effective and messes up with people's minds. Research has shown that advertising on radio and TV, which seems to be simply skipped over, becomes so ingrained in people's subconscious minds that it triggers them to buy products without them even realising why they have bought what was advertised. Information subconsciously captured in advertising settles in the brain. Giants of the world, businesses, invoke psychologists to tell consumers what to buy.

Watching TV distances you from the flow of money because when your life is shaped by TV, you become a spectator rather than a participant. It is like walking in a herd of sheep, rejecting your own needs and opinions, which makes it difficult to start living the way you want—to walk your own path. When you immerse yourself in books, especially books that stimulate consciousness and creativity, you turn to interacting with. people by motivating, you grow, and have new paths opening up. In the White Growth Studio, I teach people to live according to their heart's calling because that is a meaningful life. We do various practices, I recommend literature, and we communicate. Getting closer to our goals and continuously improving.

8. ONE SOURCE OF INCOME

All rich people have more than one source of income. These can be businesses, personal consultancy activities, hobby-based activities—and necessarily several of them, i.e., several sources of income. For example, if I am an employee, I have one source of income and depend on my employer. I seem to be living in security, earning enough money, but what if the company goes bankrupt or has redundancies? What happens to me? First, I am under a lot of stress because of the loss of my job. Second, the flow of money energy stops. Being in emotional distress, especially in low vibrations for fear for the future, distances me from success and money. I attract what I vibrate—as if I were in a vicious circle that is hard to get out of. And what happens when I have multiple sources of income? It can be an additional source of income, but very important at the time. I stay positive and can easier see the possibilities of regaining my lost source of income. My natural money energy continues to flow, more or less, but it still flows. *The habit of having several sources of income brings stability, cash flow, and positive emotions.*

9. DOING A JOB YOU DON'T LIKE

I called it a habit because a lot of people are really struggling in their work without changing anything. They get into the habit of doing things they don't like, simply serving someone else. This habit leads to another habit—constant complaining. Because when I do a job I don't like, I feel unhappy, ending up in a negative state and complaining about everything around me. People who curse their work often suppress their emotions with alcohol, nicotine, or drugs. They start celebrating the weekend on Thursday and are very sad on Sunday because the next day they will be in "hell". They get up in the morning already condemning the day ahead—it is a complete stagnation in which they suffer and degrade. There is a simple solution in this case—change a job. And if you don't know what your true vocation is, if you don't know what your mission is, you just need to find another job. Nowadays, changing careers is relatively easy. I recommend going to a job that is close to your nature, dear to your heart, and meets your needs.

10. WASTE OF FREE TIME

I often hear my clients say: "I really don't have time," "I don't know when to get everything done." When we sit down together and analyse their weekly activities and how they spend their time in general, we find about ten free hours per week with each client. Time simply wasted watching a TV series, playing computer games, chitchatting with friends, and so on. If one wants to live successfully, consciously, and in abundance, he must devote his free time to self-development, a search for activities he loves, or the establishment of useful habits—whatever enriches and fills the person. Because only a filled person (like a filled vessel) can give something to his environment; otherwise, he is depleting his resources. *In my spare time, I explore, study, search for answers, and slowly move forward.*

11. NEGLECTING HEALTH

A habit of caring about everything but your health. The habit of taking care of your health has to be the most important because your body is home to your soul. It should be healthy, clean, light, and energetic, which means a favourable environment for pursuing goals, a brighter mind, and a better quality of life. People who do not look after themselves tend to mock their healthy, strong-willed friends because that is the purpose of the human mind—to keep the person in his comfort zone. The mind protects the person and puts him on the sofa in front of the TV, because he is tired after work, allows him to stuff himself with fast food and snacks because he is in a hurry now, but will eat stewed vegetables at home tomorrow, and stretches out his hand towards a glass of beer, because there is nothing wrong with having a glass of beer sometimes, especially after a hard day. This is how the mind keeps a person in a state of self-preservation, and it is necessary to control the mind so that it serves the person rather than the person serving his mind.

Looking after one's health means exercising regularly, having medical check-ups, looking for answers to what works best for my body—exercise, massage, food, fabrics, and even furniture. I have to give everything that's best for my body and live a healthy life. If I get sick, I look for answers and watch my body. I am gradually moving towards better health—without any drastic, dramatic changes, such as jumping from eating meat to becoming a vegan—but slowly and steadily pursuing better well-being.

12. WAITING

A habit of waiting for something—a better moment, a better feeling, and when I could do THAT. I keep pushing back the date, making excuses, and letting my mind control me. Let's say it's October now, and I decided to start exercising in January. I could start exercising tomorrow, but I am waiting for the right date to start—for the 1st of January. By the way, I once asked at a sports club when their busiest time was, and I was not surprised to hear that it was January. This is because the club is full of members who have decided to start exercising at that time, but, unfortunately, they don't come back the following months, even though they have paid their annual membership fee. Waiting to do IT—to start creating, to launch own business, to read, to exercise, to earn money—is a bad habit. *It has to be done here and now.*

It does not matter that I do not know how to do it. I sit down and start looking for answers, and I find them little by little. Successful people are successful because they contribute to their success every day, even if it takes a mere ten minutes. *Stop waiting and take action every day.*

13. SELF-CRITICISM

When a person convinces himself that he lacks abilities and competences, has no talents, is constantly criticising himself (usually everywhere and all the time), and has no faith in himself, he approaches a state of fear, which is in very low vibrations—close to death. What can a person, whose vibrations and energy are at their lowest state, achieve? Nothing. He lives in a shadow, which strongly relates to beliefs developed back in his childhood. Self-critics, i.e., people with low self-esteem who pursue changes, need to see their personal achievements and praise themselves every day, even for the smallest achievements. This could even be a reply sent to 10 emails that day. Because yesterday I failed to answer them, but today I focused and did it. I am proud, praise, and reward myself. I can see my progress. This is how self-esteem is boosted—by taking small steps towards it. There are also other ways—taking courses, reading literature, and practicing. Self-doubt makes it hard to move forward and achieve goals.

14. TOXIC RELATIONSHIPS

Toxic relationships do not exist in couples only. Toxic relationship can show up equally damaging in other environments too — toxic relationships with friends, neighbours, colleagues, clients, and relatives. All the people around you who have a negative influence on my choices and drag me down. A colleague regularly inviting for a drink, a friend involving me in his family problems, an acquaintance inviting me to smoke pot, and the like. These are people who say: "Listen, why do you

need that?" or "Do you really want to do business???? Are ~~y~~
I don't see an entrepreneur in you." You have to cut all ties w~~ith~~
people. Don't try to teach or change them. Let them go, or, to be mo~~re~~
exact, remove them from your environment. If they are difficult to get
rid of (close family members, etc.), you should just ignore them—
neither see nor hear them.

Also, let go of clients who have a negative influence on you. That's
when the real change in your environment will happen—clients of a
whole new level will start coming to you. Your environment must be
clean. Once you let go of toxic relationships in your surroundings, you
begin to blossom. Your energy brightens, you radiate positivity and
peace and attract stronger and kinder people. *Once I leave toxic
relationships, I attract quality rather than quantity.*

15. HARMFUL HABITS

Harmful habits, such as alcoholism, smoking, drugs, extensive hours
spent playing computer games, overeating, not doing any sports, shut
off the flow of a person's money energy and distance him from
abundance. It is often difficult to perceive that a few nights a week with
a glass of beer or wine is alcoholism. Scientists have proven it. People
tend to justify themselves, but having bad habits prevents them from
rising up, as if putting a giant hand and pressing them to the ground.
Then entering vibrations of the money energy is impossible because, as
I have previously mentioned, it is a very strong energy, equivalent to
the energy of love. Not everyone is able to accept and retain this
energy. When people win a lottery, they go crazy having received that
much money—they buy incomprehensible things, go through hard
times, or even commit suicide. The energy of money has led to fights,
betrayals, killings at all times. In order to not only get rich but also to
retain abundance, it is necessary to completely get rid of bad habits.

...nly thing that happens in the comfort zone. ...nportant to understand that the biggest changes, ...f people, occur after having left the comfort zone. Say ... ...rs about some practice/ a course and says that he doesn't ne... ...r will take it later. It is convenient and safe for him not to take it now. Paradoxically, this is the essence of this law—a person needs to do what he fears the most because this is where the great growth of a human being has been encoded.

I see a challenge— I naturally fear it—I get out of my comfort zone and do it—I grow/improve and get results.

17. LATE NIGHTS

It's a habit of going to bed late and getting up late in the morning. The most successful people I've met in person and virtually—mentors, teachers, colleagues—get up between 3 a.m. and 5 a.m. It's really an instilled habit, my favourite one in fact, that changes the daily routine, improves the mood and gives energy. The habit of getting up early in the morning gives me an advantage over others: while everyone else is still asleep, I exercise, engage in self-development, meditate and get ready for a quality day. I have a resource of time, which I dedicate to MYSELF. This habit is the key to success, as an early bird always has the advantage.

I used to get up at 3:30 a.m. for a year. According to the Hindu teacher and mentor Sadhuru, this time of the morning is a magical time. Of course, after watching his video on getting up early at 3:30 a.m., I wanted to try, check and adapt it. One morning was enough to feel the magic of 3:30 a.m. I cannot describe the feeling—the time when all of nature is waking up has to be experienced. One year in this mode of getting up early was the most productive year of my life: I would get two days' work done in one day, coming up with really great ideas and having people and tools come to my life to implement them; this is when I had the most energy all day long and felt the healthiest. I used to go to bed between 9:30 p.m. and 10:00 p.m. Later, I gave this habit up because I immersed myself into working hard on myself—an intensive transformation and healing process took almost a year, with daily practices that required energy, which I replenished by sleeping and resting. When I change a habit, I always look at myself with love rather than forcing myself to do that with a stick. Even when I change my habit, I remain kind to myself.

All the above-listed bad habits need to be replaced with positive ones. When you act on positive habits, positive results follow—creating a quality, neat, consistent, and stimulating environment for easy growth.

CLEANLINESS

5

CLEANLINESS AND ORDER

C leanliness and order

I have already mentioned that abundance loves order. In this chapter, I will discuss in more detail why it is important to keep things tidy and clean everywhere in your life—inside of and around you.

MY INNER. MY BODY.

I want to emphasize that the changes that lead to financial success start from within. It's about how I eat, keep fit, and cleanse myself—having fasting days for my body and detoxes for my thoughts, what I breathe, and how I strengthen my body otherwise. Cleanliness of the body and soul brings me closer to discipline, gives me clarity, lightness, and allows experiences to flow through me and attract success. Daily discipline prepares the body for productive work, gives it energy, and makes leisure time and relationships with loved ones more enjoyable and fulfilling. It's all about details—what I wear, how and who I communicate with, how much I put into myself (I'm constantly learning and growing)—which add up to the whole. I become the whole, and I vibrate what is within me. Keeping the body clean and tidy, clearing out the garbage in thoughts, living in harmony with the body and the soul attracts abundance in all areas of life, especially the financial one.

MY OUTSIDE. MY ENVIRONMENT.

My outside and my environment are just as important as my inside. To attract abundance, it is necessary to get organised at:

• Home

• Place of work

• Work and personal computer

• Wardrobe

• Refrigerator

• Wallet

• Car

Home is our sanctuary. What prevails at home prevails in our life.

Disorder and chaos = discomfort, lack of money.

Order and joy = lightness, abundance, opportunities.

This is what a wide range of experts, from feng shui to psychologists, say. Rich people's homes are always kept in order. You can invest in keeping your home clean by hiring cleaning and maintenance companies, or you can organize your home yourself by developing a habit of regular tidying, putting things away, cleaning your home every season, and getting rid of unnecessary items. It is possible. And once you are financially stronger, you can share the money you earn and hire others, thus activating their job. A cleaner costs much less than people think, and certainly, the vast majority can afford to pay once or twice a month for this service to keep their homes clean and tidy.

Another important aspect is to only keep the things that make you happy. An object at home should not only have a purpose but also provide a positive emotion. You look at it, and it makes you happy! Look around carefully and inspect items—if there are any that have not been used for a long time, sitting there unnoticeable and unnecessary, get rid of them. These things just have to leave the house—they can be given away, donated, or thrown away. Unnecessary objects block the free flow of energy. Little by little, they build up, pulling people back from their own self-fulfilment. This method of cleaning up is called KonMari. Marie Kondo, a Japanese organizing consultant, has published a book and made a series of documentaries about this method of housekeeping that essentially helps to tidy up the house physically and emotionally. She recommends looking at the item, picking it up, and asking a simple question: "Does it make me happy?" If YES, then I keep the item; if NO, I donate it or throw it away. Note: just don't give junk to others! Joy is a very powerful vibration that attracts good things. So you can tell right away whether an item brings joy. If there is doubt, there is no joy. It is not the things but the emotions they evoke, which we get attached to. For example, I only have things that make me happy at home and in my wardrobe. My wardrobe has cute clothes that I enjoy wearing—at work and at home. All the clothes I wear fit me and give me pleasure. I ask the question, "Does it make me happy?" all the time—when I choose clothes, household items, jewellery, books—it has become my daily meditation.

I remember very well when I started to always keep my home clean and organized—I slowly turned it into a sanctuary. I return home and immediately get a rush of warmth and cosiness. Guests always want to stay longer here. They feel comfortable and are happy to talk on deep topics. My most apt and best ideas are born in this blessed environment —my home, which is tidy and smells good. The energy moves lightly because I clean it externally, also cleaning negative energies and then filling it up with positive ones.

I live as if I was on permanent vacation. When I am at home, I rest, find a balance, and restore my energy. *"Does it make me happy?"* is a simple and incredibly powerful question to keep asking and to keep an eye on what is coming into the environment. Women who have cultivated the archetype of a Housewife know how to conjure and give meaning to things and clothes.

It is important to note that each item must have its own place. Once you get used to putting things in their place, you don't just drop them anywhere. Even if you are in a hurry, you can always easily find them. This saves time, is accompanied by positive emotions (not being nervous about being unable to find something), and builds confidence and trust in yourself and your environment. Every object vibrates with energy and requires attention—it is given a place at home, cleaned, cared for, so to speak, constantly "in contact"—so things at home should be lovely, necessary, and bring joy.

The same principle applies to the place of work/activity. Creating a workplace that is comfortable, high quality, enjoyable and motivating. I sit down and immerse myself in the activities I have planned, creating an environment that works for me. I can work and enjoy the view from the window, listen to music, use aromatherapy (I want an activating or calming, relaxing scent)... I create everything myself and am productive. My workplace is reflected in how I treat my clients. My approach to my clients is reflected in my work results. My work results are reflected in my financial situation. My financial situation is reflected in my workplace. We can only wonder which comes first—the chicken or the egg. This does not change the point. A change to financial success starts with organising your mind and body, moving to the exterior—the image and the environment. Every last detail matters: what you eat for breakfast, what kind of car you get into, whether you've developed a habit of exercising and studying, how often you dust your desk, who you talk to, how you put your groceries in your shopping cart...

A quality life is put together like a jigsaw puzzle—and this is when joy and bliss prevail. It is a consistent and open journey of a person towards abundance. Only the most patient and open-minded people understand the laws of financial energy. I see this when I work with clients at the White Growth Studio. During the course, we cleanse the following areas: our workplace, computer, social networks, wardrobe, fridge, home, car, diet, wallet, body, thoughts, bad habits, grudges, and money energy. Having cleaned all the areas, which requires special attention, a flow of continuous abundance in all areas of life is accepted. First—cleanliness and order, inside and out, then—change and growth, success and abundance.

Both inside and out.

Outside and in.

ADDICTIONS

6

ADDICTIONS

Addictions are closely linked to the topic of habits. I've already talked about bad habits and their impact on the natural flow of money. In this chapter, I will discuss the importance of getting rid of addictions of the body and the environment in our lives, moving on to the most relevant topic—money addiction.

The Google dictionary defines addiction as the inability to stop using a substance or to refuse an act, despite the psychological and physical damage it does. *Addiction* is not just about dependence on substances such as heroin or cocaine. We can also be addicted to alcohol, a person, food, sex, money.

To be able to balance out your life, follow your dreams, and achieve quality in your environment, you need to let go of any addictions. The best place to start is your body. If I have bulimia, I start with curing it first; if I'm a smoker, I quit; if I can't live without computer games, I take steps to change that. I acknowledge my addiction, ask for help from others, take control of my body and mind, and get rid of it. This takes a lot of willpower, but once done, I gain self-esteem and self-love grow. Then it is necessary to examine our environment and let go of the addictions that arise from it—to get out of toxic relationships and manipulations, to acknowledge and change workaholism into a balanced allocation of time for work, family, and self, and to address our relationship with money—to manage our addiction to money.

When I have addictions, such as smoking, alcohol, drugs, sugar, or fast food, they are usually accompanied by financial setbacks. There are exceptions in every case, but I am talking about the majority. Now, I'm not surprised that when I had addictions myself, I did not get along with money at all. I was addicted to toxic relationships, smoked for ten years, used alcohol for 17 years, was on drugs for about 18 months, ate sugar, meat, and fast food. Addictions energetically hold back from pursuing any goals, from any growth and progress in life. Only because of strong experiences I was able to move forward, but my potential was buried under a bunch of addictions. Addictions pollute the body and the energy field, creating blocks. The blocks are like a dead weight on the body. I want to run towards my goal, but a large deadweight allows me to crawl slowly towards it. Each addiction takes away the light of life, self-love, and authenticity.

I remember a period when I drank a lot. I used to say that a glass of wine every day was no big deal. I used to buy only very good Chilean wine, deluding myself that an intelligent drink would never lead to alcoholism. I would have a glass of wine, and the tension built up during the day would subside. But with a glass of wine, I washed away not only the worries of the day but also my potential. I drowned my clear, sharp thinking, alertness, concentration, and focus in wine. After having one glass, I often craved for a second, and then there was no more planning. If I wanted to live a better life, after a few glasses, I didn't care anymore—I would just lay on the couch hoping that good life would simply happen to me, that it would come to me. But I am the one to create my life. I am the master of my own destiny. I am grateful that this realisation has come, that I have taken responsibility for everything I do, that I have given up all addictions, and that I am now able to pass on my experience to others.

What is money addiction? It is a person's ambition to solve life issues/situations with money—thinking that everything can be bought. Relying on money rather than humanity, relationships, and values. The life of a money addict is all about money—neglecting the family, fulfilling relationships, and comprehensive looking after one's body. The person loses control, and the consequences can be severe. There seems to be money, but there is nothing else—sickness, betrayals, failures, and devastating events follow.

Recognizing a person who is addicted to money is easy. Some of these characteristics dominate his life:

• he prefers compulsive money hoarding;

• shops without a purpose or pleasure (frequent emotional shopping);

• is a gambler, and engages in betting;

• seeks easy and fast money;

• buys on credit;

• often illegally hides taxes/ engages in money laundering;

• some are workaholics;

• their self-esteem is linked to the amount of money they have (a lot of money means high self-esteem, and vice versa);

• pretend that they live better lives than they really do;

• prioritise making money;

• work to earn money rather than to live and enjoy;

• do not take time for own self, for self-fulfilment (skipping lunch at work, giving up exercise, etc.);

• manipulate others and are prone to breaking promises.

The global pandemic of 2020, when the Covid virus swept across the planet and lockdowns were imposed in many countries, was a perfect illustration of how many people have an addiction to money. With the sudden closure of offices, supermarkets, bars, and restaurants, everything came to a standstill. People shut themselves in their homes, confronting themselves and their families. Of course, the psychological strain was also caused by the uncertainty of not knowing what is to come, when we will go back to our normal, ordinary life. People have gone "mad" from not being able to spend stressful days relaxing in pubs, gambling houses, and especially shopping in supermarkets. The dark side of a human being has emerged. Online trade "went crazy"—buying a lot of anything and everything. The mass buying proved that this way people wanted to satisfy their need to shop and spend money, that economists' predictions of an imminent economic crisis came to nothing. And there have been many divorces in families. The reasons are obviously interconnected: I am locked at home and severely restricted, negative emotions build up and rise, and suppressing them in the usual way is impossible - I can't go out shopping, have a drink, and socialise, I vent my emotions on the family—I lose my temper, I scold the loved ones, which leads to a family crisis. A looped chain of actions and emotions leads to destruction. Quarantine illustrated one example of money addiction.

Another example is when you want to earn a certain amount of money, and having earned it, you are not satisfied, wanting more and more. You want to have more money for the sake of having it. This is when we get caught up in a cycle of desires and actions, becoming careerists, braggarts, controllers, and losing the joy of life and sincere relationships. *Money is a consequence, not an aspiration.* It can be a goal, but it is necessary to constantly monitor yourself and your choices, or otherwise breaking free from addiction will be hard.

In my experience, I have met many people who have money in various amounts, and I can safely say that the level of satisfaction they have with their life does not depend on the amount of money they possess. Satisfaction with life depends on one's state of mind.

According to a survey by Recovery Village, 58% of those who have a heavy addiction to spending money have large debts, and 42% are unable to pay their debts altogether.

The best way to reduce addiction to money is to practice gratitude. I emphasise practice because to achieve any results with affirmations and gratitude, they should be repeated for 21 or 42 days. 21-day practices are purifying and integrating for beginners, and for advanced practitioners, this number of days is required for repeated statements to sink in. For beginners, 42 days are necessary to achieve excellent results in chanting affirmations or working with gratitude. This is what I teach at the White Growth Studio.

Gratitude is the energy of a higher consciousness level. When I forget the feelings of satisfaction and gratitude, I lose myself. Gratitude builds trust in the Source and connects me to all of Creation. By showing gratitude, I acknowledge the greatness of creative power. I also recognise the divine spark of this power that burns in every human being. Gratitude opens the true breath of life, allowing us to feel generosity, abundance, and love.

Giving up addiction requires a great deal of determination, consistency, and work on oneself. It is a constant process of self-monitoring and control until a skill to live differently is developed. And having quit all addictions, finances come as an outcome, a pleasant consequence, a source of a fulfilling life. All you need is to make a decision that you want to be independent.

EMOTIONAL INTELLIGENCE

7

EMOTIONAL INTELLIGENCE

In this chapter, I will discuss how Emotional Intelligence is related to financial success and how important it is to develop—to perceive emotions that come up, to manage them, and to feel other people's emotions. I will discuss how emotions shape a person's state of mind and why a state of mind is important when engaging in transactions, making financial decisions, organising new projects, and how to pursue satisfaction with life and experience the highest states here and now without postponing to tomorrow. The importance of the role of emotional intelligence is equated to financial intelligence. *90% of financial intelligence is emotional intelligence, and only 10% is logic.*

Emotional intelligence guides both personal life and work/business. D.Goleman argues that people with good emotional intelligence have four qualities:

• A good understanding of their emotions (self-awareness).

• They are good at managing their emotions (self-management).

• They empathise with other people's emotional experiences (social awareness).

• They are good at controlling other people's emotions (social skills).

He points out that successful entrepreneurs have high emotional intelligence. Ability/ inability to cope with one's emotions sets a person apart from others. Every day, we feel a range of emotions: fear, sadness, anger, love, hatred, frustration, joy, happiness. They often determine our decisions and choices. Successful entrepreneurs also feel the same emotions, but they don't let things go downstream, thinking about ways to improve the outcome and control the risks. The risks that come with decision-making. Focusing the intention and thoughts on risk reduction. Successful entrepreneurs do not pass on their tensions to others. They are able to control themselves and realise that this involves dealing with a certain situation that relates to a relevant issue only, and not all the areas of life. Successful entrepreneurs quickly get to know the person they talk to/their partner and act on intuition. They delve into other people's emotional experiences and anticipate their motives and behaviour.

Most people are financially unsuccessful because their emotions control their thoughts. Thoughts turn into words and actions. Actions render results. It has been scientifically proven that emotions work in the first 12 minutes. This means that once some strong emotion hits me, I need to sit down and wait for 12 minutes to pass. Whatever is left after 12 minutes can be consciously controlled to make more favourable decisions. Same emotions, but different thinking. Different thinking = different state. Different state = different actions. Different actions = different results. Thus, the biggest difference between successful and unsuccessful, happy and unhappy, satisfied and dissatisfied, etc., people is their state. These are the emotions that affect people. It is up to a person to choose how to react and to convert them.

One step towards the life you want is the state you choose. Financial success requires a change in your state of mind. By nature, everyone's soul is neutral, but the state is different! Decisions are made reflecting the state of mind. If I make a decision in a state of anger, it is likely to lead to further conflicts, disagreements, and verbal and emotional attacks. If I make a decision in a state of satisfaction, I get more of what I gave. What do I want to create? I want to create a certain financial situation. First, I define my goals and desires precisely, and then I attract exactly what I want, being in the right state of mind. Below is a scale of emotions that can be used to determine which state I am in and where I want to be.

GRATITUDE

ENTHUSIASM

SATISFACTION

INTEREST

ABSTENTION

———

LAZINESS

ANGER

HOSTILITY

FEAR, GUILT, SHAME

VICTIM MENTALITY, LOSSES

APATHY

DEATH

DEATH

Death vibration is the lowest vibration—when a person still exists, but his soul has already departed. I call them walking zombies. I see it directly—a human body walking down the street with grey, empty eyes. There is a great gap between the soul and the body, a loss of connection. Nothing happens in the state of death. The chances of raising money are zero. In this state, the person does not know what he wants out of life, and has no dreams or goals. In this state, one does not understand the meaning of life. For such people, the desire to have money sounds like an echo in deep woods.

APATHY

In a state of apathy, nothing exists for a person—he lies around a kiosk with a bottle of alcohol, living from one dose to the next, wandering around, etc., or he is absolutely frustrated with life seeing no colours in it. It's black or white all around. Everything is messed up. Such a person sits with his eyes fixed on the TV, then gets up from it and goes to work like a robot. In this state, it's common to have 6-10 glasses of beer a day and sit in front of a computer screen for days watching everything in a row. People engrossed in computer games are usually in this state.

VICTIM MENTALITY, LOSSES

In the state of victim mentality, a person sees everyone around him as bad, being the only good person. In this state, a person feels being hurt by life and others, unloved and misunderstood. The blows of life are painful, and each day is never-ending suffering. In this state, there are setbacks, disappointments, and failing goals, plans, relationships, and transactions. Bankruptcies, debts, pits of life. The state of mind—poor me, what did I do wrong to deserve this life.

FEAR, GUILT, SHAME

Fear is the biggest obstacle to success, fulfilment, inner peace, happiness, and dreams coming true. It severely weakens the immune system, leaving the physical body unable to defend itself against inflammation and serious diseases.

Common fears:

• I will fail.

• I still won't get that job or order.

• I was told NO.

• Nobody cares what I have to say.

• Too risky.

• It's not safe.

Guilt is an incredibly powerful emotion. There are many things to feel guilty about, from feeling guilty about eating a slice of pizza while on a diet to feeling guilty about having hurt someone as a child. Guilt also affects health. It leads to insomnia, loss of appetite, depression, and dissatisfaction. Prolonged guilt affects a person's self-esteem and self-worth. If a person has low or no self-esteem, he must first "unearth" what he feels guilty about.

Symptoms of toxic guilt:

• Inability to make decisions.

• Excessive sensitivity to consequences of a situation.

• Caring for others and completely neglecting own self.

• Disregarding own emotions.

People who live *in shame* feel worthless, useless, unnoticeable, humiliated. They avoid building relationships, feel vulnerable, suppress their emotions, and usually release everything through laughter. They laugh a lot until their chests explode from the accumulated pain and trauma.

The emotions *of fear, guilt, and shame* are at the bottom of the emotional scale. Very close to death vibrations. Being stuck in these emotions attracts people, objects, and events of the same vibration. So when I feel low vibrations, I sit down. I allow myself to take my time. I breathe in and out. I observe where in my body I feel that emotion. I ask where it came from and why. And after answering the questions for myself, I convert these emotions into motivation to act. I don't pity myself but rather inspire myself to take action. May your hardships inspire you to live!

HOSTILITY

A state of being stuck in a state of hostility to the environment: I am hostile to others, and as a result, I get hostility back. In this state, the environment is irritating, and the actions of others are perceived with negativity: gossip, slander, humiliation, teasing for the sake of teasing, jealousy, and contempt. This is an attempt to put oneself above others, to feel better.

ANGER

People have all kinds of experiences that leave imprints. Injuries, losses, setbacks, and other difficult events lead to a state of anger. It poisons the blood, organs, mind, and soul. People are at their most dangerous when they are angry because they take out their intense frustration on everyone they meet. They are unpredictable. In this state, positive events and progress simply don't come, and money energy runs away. Anger attracts destruction and collapse.

LAZINESS

It's an "I'll do it later" state. Laziness to take action and put the knowledge gained into practice. It is a state created by the mind's traps for self-protection—when the mind does not want to leave its comfort zone. The mind doesn't realise that there is growth; it only knows that a lot of energy will be required. So laziness is just a prison created by the mind, where an innocent human growth sits behind bars.

ABSTENTION

It is a neutral and secure state of not having an opinion, holding back, adapting, or hesitating. When a person says: "Well, I'm doing fine," "I don't care—I can go, or I can stay," "I'll be fine," etc. I feel good as it is. I call this state "Whatever"—whatever, I don't care, whatever, I don't need it, whatever, I will adapt...

INTEREST

It is a state of curiosity and discovery. A person is interested in what is behind the next door, what else he can learn, what he can do better, etc., showing interest in everything that life brings.

SATISFACTION

A state of completeness and contentment where a person appreciates and is satisfied with his environment, relationships, and activities. When I am able to enjoy everything I already have. When I am able to appreciate myself and my environment. When I am in total contentment.

ENTHUSIASM

A total passion to do, to act, and to live your life with passion.

GRATITUDE

Gratitude is the enlightenment of life. There is no greater enlightenment than being in a constant state of gratitude. In this state, everything is a success, everything goes well, the surrounding environment is great, the Universe is constantly giving gifts, and abundance is flourishing in all areas.

It is important to understand that people go through all states. The most important thing is not to stay in the states below the dash for too long. Always track and monitor your emotions. Having noticed a negative emotion, move on to a positive one. Being in emotions below the dash makes you stagnant, distancing you from fulfilling your dreams and desires, achieving your goals, and bringing on constant hard and karmic lessons. To achieve your financial goals without resistance, you need to be in the states above the dash.

The higher I vibrate, the better the results. Anything that is radiated materialises. The state you are in attracts abundance to life.

The Dalai Lama was once asked what surprised him most about humanity, and he replied: "Man! Because he sacrifices his health in order to make money. Then he sacrifices money to recuperate his health. And then he is so anxious about the future that he doesn't enjoy the present; the result being that he does not live in the present; he lives as if he is never going to die, and then dies having never lived." And this is the principle that underpins many people's lives—thinking that the future will be better and forgetting about today. The more a person has, the more he lives in illusion. Believing that tomorrow, when he buys the car he wants, he will be happy. But leasing a car becomes a burden, especially in times of financial difficulty. And then a person wants something even better than it already is. Thinking that once he has his own place, he will reach complete happiness. But then he works hard to pay the mortgage—losing financial freedom. Most people I know who own their own home are unhappy because they have other reasons to reproach themselves and others.

Many people take out a loan even to go on holiday. Then they go back to their unloved jobs and work to make up for the holidays that have already passed. And they go on holiday for as cheap as possible, saving money. And then, on holiday, they get tired of a cheap hotel, poor food, and service. They are unhappy because they will have to get back to work without resting. They check going on holiday as done, and now have something to whine about to their colleagues and friends. Since when did people start taking out loans of tens of thousands of dollars for weddings to celebrate their relationships and love? I am still amazed by this phenomenon. I haven't seen a single happy marriage that has spent huge amounts of money to legitimize it. I have seen happy marriages where people have invested their time, willingness, respect, and attention in the relationship. Most people make financial decisions based on emotions, which is why they live in total dissatisfaction. Weddings on loan are a good example of this.

In order to have a better, more harmonious, richer, more successful life, people first blame those around them and want to change everyone close to them. They don't think that what they need to do first is to look in the mirror. First, I get my relationship with myself in order and stop blaming, judging, and punishing myself. I allow life to flow through me, to experience all the emotions that I have always avoided. Let them go to make place for peace. After all, everyday life consists of what I feel, what I experience. So I clear the emotional blocks, I love myself unconditionally, and not only my parents, but everyone around me can feel it. I always remember that people around me love me as much as I love myself.

In my heart, I go back to my parents, I let go of all the grudges and anger, I apologise and thank them for life, for everything they gave and did for me, even if I don't understand or appreciate it.

I accept all that I have and go back to peace, making peace with life and allowing the Creator, the Universe, to take care of me, to love me with the warmth of other people, with favourable circumstances, and with the energy that is always flowing.

Emotional intelligence plays an important role in many aspects of daily life, including the perception of life, learning, thinking, decision-making, action, etc. It is strongly linked to financial success. Emotional intelligence can be developed, it just requires some work—listening to yourself and following your intuition, choosing the right state of mind, and seeing your surroundings.

I remain vigilant.

I accept emotions.

I control my emotions.

I am free and accept abundance.

SELF-ESTEEM

8

SELF-ESTEEM

In the chapter on a wallet, I mentioned how self-respect could be built. In this chapter on self-esteem, I will focus on how to increase and maintain self-esteem, how self-esteem relates to money, and give practical tips on how to evaluate and price your work, how to remain exceptional, and work without competition.

The Financial Capability Survey conducted in the United Kingdom in 2018 states that financial self-esteem strongly relates to a person's financial situation. The three essential ingredients for financial self-esteem are:

• Personal effectiveness—when a person believes that he can make effective financial decisions.

• Self-confidence—when a person believes in himself, acts, and executes decisions.

• Determination—when a person has the intention and the will to take control of his finances.

When these three principles are in place, people act purposefully, believe in success even when they make mistakes, and control their cash flow. Conversely, when there is a lack of confidence, lack of effectiveness, and a constant fear of making mistakes, we immerse in stagnation and apathy, losing self-esteem. Here are some of the factors that contribute to low self-esteem:

1. BELIEFS FORMED IN CHILDHOOD

I have already mentioned in the chapter on beliefs that the level of self-esteem is strongly influenced by the truths about life, values, and money shaped in childhood. These beliefs guide the decisions, choices, and judgements that people make about themselves and their environment every day. Say a child had been told over and over again that he is good for nothing, that he will never achieve anything in his life, and he starts to believe it. Such treatment becomes the basis of his self-esteem, the conviction which accompanies him through life, and often, even in favourable circumstances, when given the opportunity, he does not take advantage of it, disregarding himself. The person sees himself as a loser and doesn't even try to do anything.

2. DIFFICULT UPBRINGING

When parents constantly control a growing personality, forbidding things, suppressing curiosity or devoting little time to their children, ignoring them when they need support and encouragement, despising, and criticizing, all this affects a person's self-esteem. The person becomes obedient rather than thinking, sluggish rather than active and motivated, even aggressive because he constantly needs attention. It is the syndrome of unloved and misunderstood children, characterised by the fear of making mistakes, of being ridiculed again, of failing to meet other people's needs, forgetting one's own needs and dreams.

3. OVERESTIMATING ACADEMIC PERFORMANCE

It is often believed that performance at school will guarantee success in life. Children who do well in school are praised, parents over-emphasise their children's academic performance, underestimating their other talents. Young people with poor learning outcomes are constantly told that they will be miserable, amounting to nothing in life —their talents are suppressed and their opportunities limited.

4. FINANCIAL SETBACKS

When people experience financial setbacks, they become disappointed. It's a normal state. But while some people drown in despair, avoid critical opinions of others, and are afraid to do anything, others assess the mistake they have made, the risks they have misunderstood, and take it as a lesson. For example, in the United States, financial failures are seen positively as an entrepreneur's experience and a step towards success. In Europe, there is still a fear of financial "burns" and a reluctance to talk about them.

5. SETBACKS IN OTHER AREAS OF LIFE

It is important to mention here that mistakes are normal, and we should learn from them. I have read a book on the mastery of storytelling, which presents childhood events of famous people that had a profound impact on their life achievements. I don't remember exactly which celebrity that was, but when he was a child, his grandfather used to always ask him when he got back home from school: "Darling, what went wrong with you today? What did you learn? What did you understand?" It is the right question to ask, which develops critical thinking and shows that a failure is not a defeat. Only when we realise our mistakes and gain experience can we make significant progress.

These factors affect a person's self-esteem, and it is very bad when a person identifies his self-esteem with the amount of money. High earnings = high self-esteem. Low earnings = low self-esteem. The less money you have, the lower your self-esteem. To have more money, you need to raise your self-esteem. Improved self-esteem means more earning potential. Self-esteem needs to be stimulated. It is a circle of interactions/vibrations that needs to be understood and enabled. By taking certain actions, financial self-esteem (measured by the amount of money you have) can be raised by:

• Paying out at least one credit card, cutting it up, and closing the account.

• Earning extra income by finding hobbies and talents and monetising them.

• Refusing unnecessary purchases.

• Giving some money away / donating/ gifting it to someone in desperate need.

• Writing down all your goals and dreams on a piece of paper.

Tips on how to run your business, manage your finances and take yourself to a state of high self-esteem:

1. PUT A MONETARY VALUE ON YOUR WORK

People who start their own business/activity often provide many services for free. It even happens so that a long-standing consultant does some work—analyses, evaluations, etc.—for free. Small tasks and revisions seem to be simple and done relatively fast. But attention!!! You need to think about why you were the one asked to provide this service. Maybe you have some knowledge, skills, and experience that the client doesn't? How much time, investment, and effort did it take to become an expert in your field? Having taken all this into account and priced the work, the situation becomes clear for both the specialist and the client, doing what's good for both of them. For example, a financial company provides accounting services: advising its clients on tax planning and savings, looking into the individual situation of a company, and spending an hour or two on document review for FREE. A financial company can only do this because it has the right knowledge, and the client applies to it only because he doesn't. Everything is simple. Every task must be evaluated in monetary terms and paid. Some services can be provided free of charge, but they must be reasonably defined and limited. And again, I go back to the principle of life—I can only give when I have something to give, when I am full and filled, when I have resources. I respect my own work and time, and I respect the work and time of others. Another example comes from my client's activities. Her financial company offers a service - reduces or cancels debts/ penalties of companies. At first, she used to charge a fixed fee of £50 for this service, regardless of the penalty amount. There were cases when clients refused because the service seemed rather cheap and therefore unreliable, inadequate, and so on. It was only after three years that my client realized the uniqueness of and demand for her service and re-evaluated her work on a different basis charging a % of a penalty amount. For every penalty lifted, the company started to receive four times higher remuneration. This is a significant difference and the right decision that has given the company credibility, solvent customers, and benefit. An adequately priced service or product benefits both the seller and the buyer, boosting the self-esteem of both. I have heard the saying: If a person has never bought an expensive item, he will never sell at a high price.

2. CALCULATE HOURLY RATE

Often in a consultancy business, it is difficult to calculate your hourly rate—how to charge it to make sure that the income is satisfactory and everything is clear. I learnt how to calculate an hourly rate from one of my coaches, and I really liked this method. Let me share it with you:

• Initially, the amount of income you want to generate per year (say £100,000) is set.

• Then the amount you want to earn is divided by the number of working hours in a year - 2080 hours (or 7-8 working hours per working day). £100,000 / 2080 hours = £48 (rate of 1 working hour). Simple and clear calculations and estimated working hours.

3. DELEGATE WORK

There are entrepreneurs who try to do all the work in their company themselves—because they are the most reliable and indispensable. I don't even call such people entrepreneurs because they try to cover all the areas. They have to participate everywhere and be in control of everything. Often the business itself suffers, as it is difficult for one person to perform so many functions to a high standard. I notice that such people have low self-esteem because:

• They don't respect themselves - they spend their personal time, which should be meant for relaxation and leisure, working.

• They don't appreciate themselves - they wear themselves out by working too hard.

• They do not trust others—being too controlling of the environment and not trusting others with any responsibilities.

We need to learn how to delegate—to train people, to give them the initiative in a specific area, to accept their mistakes, and to understand that having passed certain processes, mistakes can be corrected. Then a team of trust is brought together, moving from a craftsman's mindset to the mindset of an entrepreneur. To have free time, grow your business and increase your income, you need to delegate and learn to work with others.

4. QUIT YOUR JOB IN YOUR BUSINESS

By setting up your own business, you invest money in education, gain experience working with clients, and continuously improve your work skills and competencies. When you become a master/ a specialist/ an expert in your field, you have to quit your job in your business. Train your students little by little, become a mentor, set up a training academy, organise training and start earning more. Let's say I'm a professional hairdresser, I'm well paid for every haircut I get, I have bookings three months in advance, and I earn well. That's where I stop. Because if I want to earn even more, I have to sacrifice my free time. How can I increase my income and have free time for myself? I start passing on my knowledge to other professionals (I am not afraid of competition, because there is none), I employ them, I provide training services—expanding the scope of my activities (from hairdressing to the role of a teacher/ a mentor), and I start having free time for hobbies, which can develop yet into another source of income. In a word, the hands of a craftsman/ an expert have been freed up, so it's worth quitting your job in your business to earn more.

5. UNDERSTAND THAT OTHER PEOPLE'S JUDGEMENTS ARE LIMITING

In the ups and downs of developing a business idea, a person often hears comments from others. He takes advice on what to do and what not to do and forgets his goals. He remains unappreciated and decides that it is true, forgetting his talents. Taking string consideration of opinions of others into account, he draws boundaries and loses self-esteem. I call it "being infatuated with other people's judgements." Then a person forgets what he thinks of himself and bases his self-esteem on the judgements of others.

6. BELIEVE IN YOUR UNIQUENESS AND NEED

A person with low self-esteem says: "I'm not special," "I have nothing to say," "Who cares what I know/ think," etc. He or she favours other professionals, compares himself to them, and underestimates himself. Saying that other people can give more, have advantages, and surpass him. It is good to observe the experts in your field, to study the market, but avoid "trying on their shoes" because they have different feet and different tastes—each person is authentic and needed. When a person decides that he is not interesting and unworthy of sharing his knowledge, then he refuses to help others, selfishly keeps the experience to himself, and, based on negative beliefs, lowers his self-esteem and blocks himself from being needed.

7. PUT YOURSELF IN A STATE OF HIGH SELF-ESTEEM

Self-esteem is a man-made state:

• How does it feel to be yourself?

• Do you appreciate your talents?

• Are you "comfortable in your own shoes"?

A state of feeling bad, feeling sorry for oneself, having negative personal abilities, and being afraid to express oneself is a state of low self-esteem and vibration. It is possible to enter a higher vibrational state and raise self-esteem—to praise oneself for what one has done, to appreciate every progress, to embrace every experience, and to keep remembering that one is on one's own path. Self-esteem is thus a state which can be learnt, and by constantly telling myself that I am worthy and progressive, that I am improving and striving, that I am accepting and grateful, I am putting myself in a state of high self-esteem.

8. RESPECT AND APPRECIATE YOURSELF, RESPECT AND APPRECIATE OTHERS

When it comes to self-esteem, it is important to mention the need to give up false pride. False price puts a person above others, devaluating the opinions and achievements of others. Even if I am an expert in my own field, and I highly appreciate my own achievements, I do not underestimate others in any way. I respect those from whom I learn, just as I respect those who are still on their way and still learning—we are all for all. Accepting others maintains a state of high self-esteem.

9. TURNING COMPETITION INTO A SHARING CYCLE

Competition is created by the human ego. In reality, it does not exist. A person needs another person as they are. By accepting their talents and by sharing, people create a circle of dissemination—turning competition into a cycle of sharing. For example, I have a finance company in the UK that helps Lithuanians living here with their financial affairs. There were many similar accounting and bookkeeping companies before me. I joined the market without thinking that I would be competing with someone else. I watched each of the Lithuanian accounting firms, admired some, learning from others how not to do or how I do not want to do—I simply researched. Today, I work relying on my values and principles without competition. I have my clients come to me, and others have theirs. We all use the principle of choice based on values, price, and time. There is enough for everyone, with exchanges and sharing of information and services. I encourage you to go your own way, to be authentic, and to work without competition.

Thus while self-esteem starts to develop in childhood, it is possible to continuously build it, to achieve and maintain a state of high self-esteem, and thus attract financial success and opportunities.

I stop comparing myself to others.

I reject competition.

I am unique.

I am needed.

I know my worth.

I accept the flow of money meant for Me.

EGO

9

EGO

I n this chapter, I will discuss the role of the ego in pursuit of making as much money as possible (when money becomes the goal) and the ability to respect your nature, to act out of your calling, to fulfil yourself by creating value for people, and to earn (when money becomes the result).

Everyone comes into this world for a purpose. I have talked about this in other Chapters. Here I want to talk about ways to plan work/activities dear to your heart that bring satisfaction and abundance, and ways to avoid the human ego's desire to live a rich but empty life without fulfilling own mission, working hard, and chasing after other people's opinions.

For the energy of money to circulate smoothly, *money must, first of all, come as a result, not as a goal*. People must want to add value and fulfil their talents. Some talents people bring with them at birth and acquire others through socialising, studying, and working. Every experience shapes the personality. People have a clear purpose—the added value they can bring to others. Some do it by giving advice, others—by making things, yet others sell, educate, and give hugs. All that matters is that such activities bring joy and are valuable to others. *You have to feel complete satisfaction in your work— I work, and I do not feel it because I do it all with ease.* This is self-fulfilment/ mission/ purpose. Because when my EGO intervenes, all I do is fight to earn as much as possible. For example, an entrepreneur, who opens a café, thinks about his customers—making sure they are happy and comfortable enjoying delicious food, creating a positive working atmosphere. All this is very important: creating value means satisfaction and money. When opening up a café, if an entrepreneur thinks about "making" a lot of money, skips important preparatory stages, disregards work ethics, hides taxes, and ignores customer feedback, this brings a surge of negative energy. Neither customers, nor staff, nor the founder feels any pleasure out of that, even though they are earning a lot of money. It is not the amount of money, but the way in which it comes, that matters most. Unfortunately, many sell their souls for money, participating in the rat race, because they want a piece of cheese—they become slaves to money and forget the natural nature of money energy.

Countless businesses fail because they are motivated to make a profit rather than to add value for as many people as possible. It is only a fear of doing what one's heart truly desires that hinders one's true self-fulfilment. A person without a passion for the activity and a conscious choice of his path is far from his true self. Such entrepreneurs/ specialists/ experts can be easily identified:

• a hairdresser with greasy, bad looking hair,

• a dentist with crooked teeth,

• an obese dietician,

• a financial specialist who has debts,

• a chef who cooks for vegans and eats meat himself,

• a vet having no love for animals,

• a doctor who is always ill,

• a lawyer who can't handle his own affairs,

• a coach who teaches about relationships but does not have a partner or harmonious relationships.

All these people do these jobs because they are paid money to do it. They will not give any satisfaction to customers in the services they receive because they are dissatisfied with themselves.

For a long time, we have been told a lie that we have to work for money, that money, fame, career, other people's love, good reputation, and recognition is all that matters. I have to do something to get something. It's something that has been drilled into us by our parents since childhood: "You can go out after you do the dishes," or "If you clean the floors for a month, we will buy you a bike," etc. This kind of parenting shifts a person's motives from intrinsic to extrinsic ones. The innate desire to improve, create, do, and be happy is lost. Ultimately, many people cannot find a single area of life that would be satisfying to them. People do jobs they don't like, establish businesses that become a burden, maintain unfulfilling relationships, even take holidays they don't really want. They do all this just to comply with social norms. So I ask myself: whose life am I living?

To find the answer, I have to dare to choose my inner call for change and decide to be happy. I ask myself again: "What kind of work would I do even if I wasn't paid for it?" Having honestly answered this question, I get a sense of what activities would bring me closer to true happiness and plenitude. Choosing your true vocation is important—then money will come in an easy natural flow, you will fall in love with the being, with people, and with yourself.

What I mean is that money is a by-product of meaningful work. Now is a perfect time, given as a blessing by the Universe, to deal with our neglected psychological state, to truly fall in love with ourselves, to let go of everything that is leaving, engaging in meaningful, value-adding activities that bring happiness to ME first and foremost.

I notice that the pursuit of wealth has made people soft and weak-willed. Many feel privileged to become rich without any effort - they dream of making a million because it has become a socially acceptable aspiration. Everything seems fine with that. But most people chase the mythical million without realising that it is not even necessary for a full-fledged life, that living with much less and the way one wants is possible.

As long as the goal = a million, I set a hostile example for my children and teach them vanity.

As long as the goal = a million, the path of abundance is through stray.

As long as the goal = a million, the soul is lost in karmic processes.

As long as the goal = million, true self-fulfilment and mission are abandoned.

First, a person needs to refine his dreams and visualize them— write them down, draw them, and make a collage of them. I recommend, in particular, writing down on a piece of paper exactly what I want, what I need, and what I pursue. When a person wants a million of dollars and knows exactly how he will use it, he sends a message to the Universe. We need to clearly word our goals so that the million can come—money comes when there is a goal for it to come. Write down amounts in figures which you plan to spend in one way or another, e.g., to pay off a debt of £100,000, buy a house for my parents for £231,800, etc. When a message with specific numbers and goals, which are not taken out of the blue, are not illogical (e.g., it is not that I am sitting in front of a shed and suddenly realise that I want a yacht), but are measured and planned, is sent to the Universe. The opportunities come, and the Source opens up.

In reality, a million is just a number—neither big nor small. I give meaning to that number myself.

I remember many years ago, I went to a picture framing workshop. Its owner was shabby, constantly smoking, and a rather unattractive man with half of his teeth knocked out. But he was a man with his own charm and values. I mentioned to him that I loved Shoreditch, but it is an expensive district and buying a house here for less than a million is impossible. He turned to me with a calm, unchanging face and said: "And what is a million? That's nothing." He radiated a steady peace. I wondered back then that such an apparently simple man had such a mindset. I carried that meeting in my mind for a long time and kept going back to it. Then I realised that a million is just a perceptual limit created in my own mind. If I don't give importance to the amount of money, then there is no limit to earnings.

A successful person is not measured by the millions which he earns. A successful person is someone who knows what he wants and how to get what he wants and who lives the way he wants to live—without compromise.

A successful person is one whose source of abundance is alive. He drinks from that source himself, giving 10% to others.

A successful person is one who is in a constant state of satisfaction with his life.

A successful person is one who is able to see the lessons of life, to say goodbye to people whom he learnt his lessons from on time, and to neatly untie karmic relationships.

A successful person is a humble disciple.

A successful person wakes up and goes to sleep with gratitude.

Forget templates. Wake up to your life. May creativity, patience, and love be with us!

SAVING MONEY

SAVING

PURPOSEFULLY SETTING MONEY ASIDE (SAVING)

People tend to save money. I recommend replacing the word "save" with "set aside" because to save means to try not to spend money, to put it aside, to accumulate it—as if to live in fear, refraining from spending (a negative connotation is perceived in the meaning).

To set aside money—to put it aside for a specific purpose. *Setting aside money having a specific purpose for spending it is essential.* This could be a new car, a vacation, studies, a financial cushion, etc. Never save money for a rainy day. Please, anything but a rainy day. When you save for a rainy day or an emergency, the rainy day or the emergency ALWAYS comes, and money runs away. This is basic event programming. Money stays only when saving for a purpose. There are countless cases of grandmothers stuffing money under the mattress, in their socks, hiding it under the floor—for a rainy day that will come. It all ends with scammers and thieves coming and robbing them. Sometimes the money is misappropriated by relatives. In all cases, moral and sometimes even physical harm is suffered. This is just one example, but I have to admit that intimidated by rising prices, the virus that has taken a grip on the world, the geopolitical situation, people save money for that bad day, which eventuality comes.

Often my clients share their experiences of saving money but not being able to save because of all sorts of unforeseen events—either a car breaking down, a leaky roof, a sickness of a loved one. Various misfortunes do not allow them to save. When I ask them, "What are you saving for?" the answer I usually get is "I save for such hardships." So what else can we expect?

My advice is to set aside a percentage of your salary each month and transfer it to another account. This way, your savings will be kept separately, avoiding the possibility of accidentally spending that money on something else. I notice that the same attraction/ vibration sequences apply in the law of saving—I attract what I save for. That's why it is important to pay attention and set the right goal—to save for a thing, an event, a trip, education, real estate.

I set money aside for my dream.

FINANCIAL CUSHION

I have already mentioned that money can be set aside for *a financial cushion*. What does this mean? A financial cushion does not mean money set aside for holidays, things, entertainment, or something else. It means an amount of money enough to live on for six months at the least without working. This money comes in very handy when you change jobs, decide to quit a job, engage in an activity you love, or move to another city, etc. Then you can start with a financial cushion, which is calculated as follows: counting all your necessary monthly expenses and multiplying them by 6. These savings are sacrosanct - not to be used for any other purchases!

A financial cushion means savings to live on for six months.

EDUCATION IS THE BEST INVESTMENT

Investing money in education, self-education, and self-development is the best way to go. This is something you have to let yourself do without saving it. Investing in yourself pays off tenfold, which is why setting money aside for education is one of the best choices.

When I started on my self-development path, I used to watch various free videos. Then I attended several free seminars and workshops. Finally, I started buying inexpensive, short courses; the price I paid slowly went up, and trainings got longer as my thirst for knowledge grew with it. Today, I can confidently invest in a course that lasts a few months, paying £10,000 for it. I have chosen a gradual system of investing in myself instead of setting aside money for my education. The more I invested in my knowledge, the more return I got. The returns came in many forms: money, appraisal, a new project proposal, meeting interesting and influential people who opened up even more opportunities. From then on, it was up to me to decide which opportunities to take and whether to take them at all. My path of abundance has unfolded in a wonderful, beautiful, delicious way, with great gifts. I feel blessed to have invested in self-education because it has opened up a whole new world. My life has become complete—a blessed life of abundance and prosperity.

FOCUS ON YOUR HEALTH

I note that taking care of your health is necessary, without saving at the expense of it:

• allow yourself to eat fresh, balanced, minimally processed food;

• drink enough water;

• detoxify your body (preferably with the help of a specialist);

• pamper your body with massages and various wellness treatments;

• get a good rest and comfortable night's sleep;

• exercising outdoors or at a sports club;

• go swimming;

• buy comfortable footwear and wear fabrics made of natural fibres;

• spend more time outdoors - in the fresh air;

• give up alcohol, smoking, and other harmful habits;

• Take time for yourself - meditate, pray, or spend at least an hour a day being with yourself.

People who advocate a healthy lifestyle would probably add a few more points, which is welcome. Because, like you, I am still in search of the best, the most suitable for ME, for MY BODY. I listen to my body all the time: when I'm full of energy, when I want to take a nap for at least 20 minutes, when I'm craving fresh fish in the supermarket, and when I get a sore neck working on my computer. I am constantly talking to my body, testing it, looking after it, and then I am rewarded—by being healthy, light, thoughtful, energetic, and relaxed. Definitely, looking after your health costs—I avoid saving on my health. Because taking care of health pays off in the long run—retaining body mobility, enjoying life more, delaying old age, and avoiding disease.

Setting aside money, investing in your health and education, and building a financial cushion are all welcome steps towards progress, planning, decision-making, and abundance.

I set money aside with a purpose.

I attract what I save for.

I avoid the mistake of simply hoarding and preserving money for no purpose.

I take care of my health and invest in it.

The best investment is my education, my self-development.

DEBTS

DEBTS

The International Institute of Finance estimates that global debt rose to a record \$258 trillion in the first quarter of 2020. And the debt continues to grow.

The average person lives with a debt of around €38,000 on a regular basis, not including the mortgage. I want to point out that being in debt is not an innate human nature. Our natural human nature and aspiration is to live in abundance—our own natural flow of abundance. So what should we do with our debts?

This chapter will distinguish between good and bad debts, how and why debts must be paid back, how to borrow (lend) money, and when to lend (borrow) it.

If someone asked me if I had debts, my answer would depend on my understanding of the word "debt". Theoretically speaking, debt is something (usually money) that needs to be repaid. If I borrowed money for a weekend of fun, that's a debt too. By treating it differently, I create an illusion and lie to myself. I see a bank loan as a debt that I have to repay, or else I will suffer—losing my property or business. So debts come in many forms.

GOOD DEBTS

There are debts/ loans that today's people cannot do without. Most people find it difficult to pay for their housing or education in full, so they take out a loan, and the money borrowed helps them achieve their goals. If properly measured and assessed, it could be a mortgage, education, or business loan.

Also, in certain emergency situations, debt can be a sensible and often the only option. For example, if your washing machine breaks down, buying a new one on leasing may be cheaper than saving for six months. I always calculate—how much extra time will I have to spend on various chores, how many difficulties will I have? How much extra time will I lose if I hand wash for the next six months? What works will I have to sacrifice to set aside the required amount? I analyse the situation and borrow because it is the right thing to do.

When I borrow money in any category, I first make sure that I am borrowing to create long-term positive results for myself and my family. This is the basis of good debts.

BAD DEBTS

Debts start to work against you when they are used to pay for things you could do without and which you definitely cannot afford (for example, a holiday to Thailand!). There's nothing wrong with buying something just because I want it, but first, I make sure I can afford it. *The intention with which I borrow money is very important.* When the intention is empty—say, to buy clothes, knick-knacks, to show off, or for a short-term lull—then the money falls as into the Bermuda

Triangle and disappears. Bad debts are other people's money spent frivolously.

HOW TO REPAY DEBTS?

The first step to managing debt is to take responsibility. Borrowing money = paying it back. When I borrow, I know it's not my money, and it can't stay with me. I always borrow other people's money and pay back my own. This makes it difficult to repay debts. Unconscious consumption/ buying has led most people to bankruptcy, psychological problems, even suicide. There is a growing tendency to run away from debt altogether—avoiding commitment and responsibility. This means I'd rather go bankrupt than pay my debt back, even if it's not big and can definitely be repaid. Bankruptcy is only declared as a last resort when the situation is really, really bad. Although I always say: there is a way out of every situation. Always. All you have to do is to immerse yourself in the analysis, learn and *do something*. Knowledge alone does not produce results, action = result.

When I take responsibility and start to pay my debts, the qualities of honesty develop and grow in me. I am strengthening myself as a person because I give back responsibly what does not belong to me. It is important to pay a debt back as soon as possible because then I pay back less money—the longer the term, the bigger the overpayment (I pay more interest). Paying back faster = giving away less. Sometimes people pay high interest rates without even realising it—as high as 40-50%. They pay monthly instalments, and their debts do not decrease, sometimes even increasing. I recommend structuring the maturity of a debt and setting a deadline for repaying it. This will bring clarity and the awaited moment of victory. If you find it difficult to do it yourself, I can help you with debt repayment—we have one-to-one sessions at the White Growth Studio for this.

HOW DO I BORROW (LEND) MONEY?

Debt needs to disappear from my life altogether because when I lend/ borrow money, I connect myself energetically to that person. As long as I am indebted to a person, we are connected. As long as a person is indebted to me, we are connected. It all is interconnected. I heard a story about two friends, one rich and the other always struggling with money. He asked a friend to lend him money. The rich friend replied: "I don't want to lend you money, because when you call me, I will think that you are calling to pay me back, and you will not do that but will invite me to a bar. Then I will think about why you are going to the bar with me, if you owe me money, and I will be disappointed in you. But you will probably not invite me to a bar yourself because you will be afraid to call me—you are indebted to me after all! And our friendship will end, we will ruin our relationship. I'd rather give you this money!" This story is a small example of how a lender and a borrower are linked in a relationship that is often negative.

It is very important to always lend money with interest and with a time limit for repayment—even if you are lending to family members. I show respect for myself and lend with a 10% interest at the least. This obliges a person, as he has to give back some of his money—not only what he has borrowed, but also the interest. People feel a sense of responsibility and added value. When they know they have to pay back £20 or even £100 more than they borrowed, they weigh up whether it's worth borrowing at all and feel gratitude and satisfaction when they pay back the debt. This creates a positive connection and a better vibration in terms of money energy building a relationship with money. When I lend money without a time limit for repayment, without interest, I am consciously aware that this money can turn into charity. Once I realise this, I understand if I want to lend money at all. If I know I may not be able to recover the money I borrowed, then I need to either:

• refuse to lend money altogether to avoid negative feelings towards the person;

• or to give it with the intention that I am donating this money.

When I lend money to friends, my family, or colleagues, I remember to be generous to myself. This means that I, first of all, lend money when I have it, rather than out of pity. I have the resources to lend. Then I am generous to others because I help. I'm generous to myself because I don't have to take the shirt off my back to help others.

IT'S WORTH LIVING DEBT-FREE!

It is possible to live debt-free! This is a fact that I have experienced myself. And that is a great feeling. I know what it's like to be in constant debt - I had £60,000 in debt. Like most consumers, I used to love using credit cards—buying nice clothes, dining out in restaurants. I allowed myself to live pleasantly but unconsciously. If I want it, I buy it, even if I don't really need it. This continued for almost five years. I didn't realise at the time that I was harming myself. I paid my instalments every month, but my debts didn't go down—I was like a squirrel in a cycle of debt. It's very hard to get out of it, but it's worth it. After analysing everything and structuring a plan, I cancelled my £60,000 debt in 9 months. I am now completely debt-free! And I wish everyone the same!

To summarise, I want to emphasize that the most important thing is the intention—knowing the purpose for why I lend or borrow. In both cases, I have to respect both my own and other people's money. Because the way I treat the money I earn, it will treat me the same. The law of absolutes: I get what I give. What goes around comes around.

DONATIONS

DONATION

The law of charity speaks of a simple principle—I will only share with others when I am full and have something to share and give 1 0% of what I receive.

A person is implementing his activity/vocation/mission and receives money as a result, i.e., he earns money. According to the effective laws of money energy, a person must share his profits, giving 1 0% to charity. Here I would like to note that when you share it right, money always comes back. 1 0% given = 1 0% getting back (sometimes even more). A container always fills up. Charity can also be giving your time for something, for example, sharing your knowledge with others, volunteering, or helping out in various ways. This intention comes from fullness. If more than 1 0% goes to charity, that's fine, as long as it does not come out of your reserve. I share with others when I am full, when I am financially stable, when I have resources, when I feel comfortable, and when I live in fullness and natural abundance. Otherwise, when I try to give without having, I break the energetic laws of money, which leads to negative consequences: I lose motivation, energy, inspiration, connections, and other important elements. *The Universe rewards those who value themselves and help other people.*

When I was in India, one of my spiritual guides gave me a sacral life chart that came from ancient Indian scriptures:

Vidhhya Dadaati, Vinayam Vinayati Yati Patratam Patratvat Dhanamapnoti Dhanati Dharamam Tatah Sukham.

This scheme of life has strongly impressed me and "stuck" to me, I see it as the essence of the principle of life, and I follow it. It goes from top to bottom and I will explain how it works:

KNOWLEDGE

DISCIPLINE

MY VESSEL

MONEY

CHARITY

HAPPINESS

KNOWLEDGE

Knowledge is the first step in the scheme of life. People live and accumulate knowledge—first by growing up naturally, learning about their environment, then by going to school, studying, and then deepening their knowledge in their chosen field. It is human nature to learn and grow. You shouldn't think that you can stop when you leave school or university. Learning is continuous and lifelong. This should be the aspiration of any individual. There are all kinds of things to learn (and I don't just mean spiritual things)—you have to learn to cook soup too! All knowledge is useful and necessary, just as every human being is necessary and has a purpose. Whatever the path you choose, it is a path walking which you constantly fill yourself with knowledge.

DISCIPLINE

Discipline is brought into play when knowledge has been accumulated and needs to be put into practice. Discipline helps make theory tangible. There are many people (I call them know-it-alls) who know everything but don't put that knowledge to any use. Unused knowledge is worthless. Knowing is all that is left—that is where it stops. Without moving up the ladder, there is a sense of stagnation and being stuck in many areas: self-fulfilment, finances, relationships. When knowledge stays in the head, money energy stops. To be disciplined means to do your part, to use knowledge to create value. When discipline is connected to knowledge, action is taken, and ways are found to fill oneself up.

MY VESSEL

Here I move on to the next step in the scheme of life—*my vessel*. I accumulate knowledge, I bring discipline into play, I do my part, and thus fill my own vessel. I do not go around giving myself to everyone and everywhere while I am just an empty vase. I have nothing to give— I am an empty vessel. Let's say I want to pour some soup for someone to share with him, but there is no soup in my vessel—it is empty. How can I offer something to someone when I have nothing to give? Whether it's my spouse, employer, or someone else, I just can't share because I am empty. The same principle applies to both material and spiritual things. Therefore, in order to move towards the fullness of life, I have to fill myself up, and I have to choose how to do it. There are many things that can fill a person up with, including:

- laughter

- various spiritual practices

- dancing

- singing

- cultural events

- meetings with family and friends

- physical work

- sports

- walks in the nature

- travel...

It's important to feel what charges me up and how it affects me. Am I an introvert or an extrovert? Melancholic or expressive? What is my priority role in life? What is my archetype? I am filling up in the most appropriate and acceptable way for me—I feel very good, I am in a high vibration, and I attract processes through which I can share. A full vessel is a necessity if you want to move towards money.

MONEY

A person has accumulated knowledge, has the discipline to use it, has filled himself up, and now is a full vessel, and then the next process happens—*money comes naturally*. He attracts money, energy and can easier earn money. When I am a know-it-all, or even ignorant and show no interest, when I have no ambition and no discipline, and when I am an empty vessel, money simply does not reach me. Then I have to work hard for a living, I give up my dreams and lose faith, I fall into low vibrations—my window of vision is very narrow. In this state, I move away from money, and it is very difficult to re-engage with it. Therefore, it is important for money to become the result of activity/sharing.

CHARITY

When a person is able to earn, his abundance energy is open and moving, and he can engage in *charity*, i.e., give from his surplus. This is when the law of charity, which is a very important law of money energy, comes into play. If a person gives when he has little, he usually gets payback through health problems or being cheated. There is a reason why this step is the penultimate one—charity is not given in the first place. It does not start with charity; it is only empowered having passed other steps in the chart of life. I have inserted this life chart in the chapter on the law of charity so that people understand that engaging in charity is only possible when one has spiritual and material resources

HAPPINESS

Happiness is the final stage, the fulfilment, the satisfaction of being. It comes from having passed all stages in the chart of life. When a person has knowledge in a chosen field (it can be a profession, parenting, gardening—any field one likes) when he puts that knowledge to good use, when he knows the ways and is able to replenish himself to stay in high vibrations, when the flow of money comes naturally—through self-fulfilment, through activities one loves, and when he gives some of his wealth to others out of fullness and gratitude to the Universe, then a feeling of plenitude and happiness comes.

This chart of life perfectly combines the stages of maturity, of moving towards abundance, without skipping any important step or swapping places. It reveals the sequence of actions and shows how important it is to give charity when you already have enough, living in natural abundance. This chart has been 100% successful for me, so I am teaching other people to follow it as well. I share because I see a value in it and because I already can.

ASTROLOGY AND KARMA

13

ASTROLOGY AND KARMA

KARMA

Everyone comes into life with karma. Depending on how a person has lived in past lives, his karma is more or less clean. How does karma relate to money? Here I would like to point out that a person's financial situation depends on a variety of factors—beliefs, lifestyle, emotional intelligence, as well as a karmic relationship with money, which can be improved, worsened, or maintained as it was when he was born.

There are four patterns of behaviour that determine a person's karmic passport, their karmic relationship with money, and thus determine the success/failure of many other areas of their life. Because karma is the consequence of past lives and present life right/wrong treatment of people, money, and oneself.

1. *When a person is born with clean karma and maintains a positive karmic relationship with money,* he is usually referred to as a 'born lucky'. He lives in abundance, is often in a good position to make

money, and is "clean" with people and money. The result is abundance, success in relationships, and no major health problems.

2. *When a person is born with clean karma and spoils it by having a negative relationship with money*—robbing, cheating others, not paying, making illegal money deals, etc., then the consequences boomerang back in various areas of life. Relationships, health, and unwanted painful events may be affected.

3. *When a person brings bad karma with him and lives in a right way with others, with money,* then he cleanses the karma, redeems it. Suppose that in his past life, a person engaged in machinations, embezzled money, evaded taxes, defrauded somebody, or cheated on a lot of people, and he did not realize that, showing no repentance in that life, then his karma carried over to the next reincarnation. It means that in this life, such a person must treat money with the utmost respect and fairness.

4. *When a person brings bad karma with them and further tarnishes it through illegal financial practices,* then destructive processes often occur, and karma hits him hard—through a severe illness, painful losses, and constant money losses. Karma does work, and when we bring it from our past lives, it works even faster and is more painful.

Karma is, therefore, the result of a person's thoughts, words, and actions, the result of a way of life. Sometimes a friend's or a relative's life seems to be in harmony (positive relationships, good health, orderly finances), and suddenly life unfairly punishes him (some painful events happen), it is important to realise that nothing happens for no reason. Every consequence has a cause. Perhaps he is atoning for sins of his past life, or perhaps he has managed to "do his bit" in this one. I pay special attention to correct behaviour on the financial level, which is often overlooked but is very important for the creation of a clean karmic relationship with money and for human destiny in general.

ASTROLOGY

Human existence is not only determined by karma but also by the position of the planets. Astrology can tell us what karmic consequences a person must face and what his vocation and mission in life are. In this chapter, I want to stress that by knowing oneself, by looking into one's talents, one's given and developed qualities, one's habits, a person can maximize one's potential and live this reincarnation to the fullest in a fully productive, happy way.

Who am I according to the Human Design System?

Who am I according to Evolution or some other cognitive system?

Who am I according to astrology, according to the alignment of the planets?

What is my Soul Plan?

Knowing your own self is absolutely necessary in order not to go against yourself.

What has self-knowledge given me? When I found out what karma I carry from my past reincarnations, I understood how to deal with certain situations. For example, my astrology says that I must be very responsible with money and do good deeds. I saw it as a personal responsibility and helping someone else. To help others and to do something good, I have to allow myself to earn money. To give, I must first receive. I have to earn through Truth.

I was very curious to know myself through the alignment of the planets, to find out the traces of my past reincarnations, and I made sure to take advantage of the answers I got. Later, working with various clients, I have seen many karmic lessons that have taken place, and I have heard all sorts of stories and incidents related to money energy and karmic money connections. I remember one of my clients made an astrological money chart and found out that he had been involved in money machinations in a past life. I thought that this information had reached him in time because if he continued in this life with the same inspiration, it would affect his health, he would have accidents, and continuously lose money. We talked about it and discussed how to clear karma and improve money relations.

I once had a new client come to me for accounting advice. He was quite open about the fact that he always ends up having a bad employer. His last employer also cheated him. A client did a project for £40,000 and wasn't paid for it. Other employers have also cut corners, paying out less than the full amount. I listened attentively and asked him one question only: "Roland, why do you keep underpaying your employees?" He even leaned back in his chair, looked at me with big eyes, and asked: "How do you know that?" and then added: "And what does this have to do with me?" I explained how everything is related. It was very obvious to me what was going on in his situation and where the roots of the problem were.

What have I learnt from working with clients? I have to listen to them, apply all my knowledge and experience, and help them. This is how I still carry out my mission—to do good works and open a channel of human abundance. All people have a channel of abundance. Beliefs, blocks, karma, or poorly aligned planets can stop the natural flow of money energy. According to astrology, it is important to know that one person can make money easier, another finds it harder, one will have plenty and some, while another will have only as much as he is worth and no more. The third will have money come through hard work and effort—through extensive investments in himself and his activities. It is human resilience that allows us to achieve our goals. There are some people whose self-fulfilment has been determined by stars to be achieved in their forties. Knowing this information can help you not to agonize, understanding that there is no need to compare yourself with a friend who has already started acting and earning money. So, depending on what a person's central planet is, where it is located, how it interacts with the other planets, abundance comes into one's life at different times, in different ways, and in different quantities:

• Money is easy to earn—a smooth flow of money energy (here, karma must also be clean).

• Money is earned through hard work, great effort, and human resources.

• Money is earned only to the extent of what a person is worth, and no more.

So it is important to know what your central planet is. Each planet determines a unique relationship to money:

Mars
The owners of this planet are those people who have a tremendous passion for achieving goals to keep moving forward. They do what they love and become extremely successful. They have a great potential to attract money to their life.

Venus
This planet can reveal abilities to attract money. They have a great potential to attract abundance to their life through creativity.

Jupiter
Fortune, luck, abundance, and development. They have a great potential to attract money to their life.

Neptune

Unlimited abundance, particularly good at attracting money through manifestation.

Saturn
Potential for stability and fixed assets.

Pluto
Big money and karmic money lessons.

Uranus
Sudden ups and downs at the financial level, frequent surprises in personal finance.

An astrologer can help you learn about the alignment of the planets and their impact on your life, calling, and mission. Attention! Choose the right astrologer—a professional, a practitioner, who has a good intuition and relies on his gut feeling. Such professionals also give personal sessions, go deep and give value. I have met many astrological theorists, who would send me loads of material without explaining, leaving me to study it by myself, who take a superficial approach to their work, are in low vibrations themselves, and often cheap. Stay away from them because they are a waste of your money. Get a personal feel for which professionals are masters in their field, and look into their activities.

White Growth Studio helps people set up their soul plan, including the astrological money path. And when you clear up astrological questions, when you know what is given to you by the stars, what is your highest potential, what is the direction that allows you to go easy, to fulfil and to earn, what activities, in general, you can come to abundance in, then you can empower your talents, competencies, and skills to develop the activities you love, to give value to other people and to earn money.

RELATIONSHIP WITH FATHER

14

RELATIONSHIP WITH FATHER

This chapter will look at how a person's life is affected by their relationship with their parents and why it is important to re-establish a good relationship with your dad—a direct key to self-fulfilment and abundance. I will give you valuable insights from my teacher Milda Sabiene, who is a professional in this field.

Relationships with parents are the foundation of a person's life. Relationships with parents determine the quality of life. For example, the relationship with mother is responsible for relationship with the other half. If a couple's relationship does not go well, the first thing to do is to sort out the relationship with the mother. If a person's financial situation is in flux—ups and downs (having money, and then having none)—then the first thing a person needs to do is re-establish his relationship with dad. The relationship with dad is a reflection of a person's financial situation and a path to self-fulfilment.

A supportive, good relationship with parents does not necessarily mean frequent visits, face-to-face or telephone contact. This is a fundamental, general feeling towards parents—what do I feel about them? Are there any grievances and reproaches remaining from childhood? Do I remember rejection or lack of love? Maybe I had particularly difficult childhood experiences—physical or psychological abuse, sexual harassment? What is the state that comes to my mind when I think of my parents: lack or fullness, reproach or gratitude, indifference or care? Most adult children have grievances with their parents about their childhood experiences, which they vibrate in adulthood or withdraw from their parents altogether. Even children who have grown up in a close-knit family with warm and close relationships have grievances against their parents—bigger or smaller, but they do. There's even a popular saying: "Grandparents, love and spoil your grandchildren, as they will take revenge on your children..." It reflects the sad truth that children constantly reproach their parents. So how do I, as an adult, re-establish a good relationship with my parents? Because *having a good relationship with your parents means not holding grudges and resentments against them. It means understanding them.*

Main 5 steps to help you to accept your parents, to re-establish a positive relationship with them:

1. *I have to understand that I had all my childhood experiences because my soul chose to come into the world through this (my) dad.* It is my own choice. All the events and experiences have been given to me to make me stronger and to create the life that I am living or potentially can live because I choose growth and opportunities rather than a victim position.

2. *I have to understand that my dad doesn't/didn't specifically wish me ill.* My dad went through very difficult experiences himself, which is why he treated me the way he did. What did my dad have to go through not being able to love, to show love? He may have experienced violence, rejection, and abuse. It's like a vicious circle—if my parents

are abusive towards me, they have probably suffered even more abuse from their parents. Knowing how difficult it was for my parents—living in ignorance and dark because they did not have this information—I have a responsibility to myself to take off these burdens of deliberation, comparisons, doubts, and unfulfilled expectations.

3. *I need to understand that if my dad did not love me the way I wanted him to or the way I understand love, he loved me the way he could and the way he was meant to love.* Dad hasn't experienced love, so he doesn't know it, doesn't know how to express it in other ways. Perhaps he sees love as providing the essentials for children: a home, food, clothing. He doesn't know what it means to hug and cuddle. Maybe in stressful situations, my dad snaps, and I feel guilty about everything that's going on around me—but not having self-control doesn't mean having no love. I reproach a person and ask him to do things he does not know and cannot do. I have to stop complaining and accept my dad's love for me.

4. *I have to thank my dad/parents for everything they have given me in this life.* Thank them over and over again. Not to forgive, but to thank!!! First, for being the source through which I came to life. Life is the greatest gift my parents gave me. Secondly, my parents did absolutely everything, with all their hearts, that was best for me and the best they could give. If they didn't do as I expected them to, they did the best they could do. They had nothing else to give, nor did they have to. There is no such thing as something that parents must give.

5. *I have to apologise to my parents that I, as an adult child, could not understand them—their pain, their experiences, and their traumas.* Preparing for the moment of apology is necessary, having practices created specifically for that, and the result will be astonishing. Humility before parents changes people's lives profoundly, I have seen it in my clients' experiences, and I have lived it myself.

My dad was a malignant narcissist and a man with an oppressive behaviour. He used to harm animals without mercy, and he was violent towards my mother and brothers. I remember my dad banging my mum's head against the wall and physically trying to throw her off the 5th-floor balcony. He sexually assaulted and harassed me and many other women as well. While I was living with him, I saw violence, screaming, shouting, blood, my mother injured, my brother abused, and I experienced a great deal of anxiety, stress, fears, and instability. I used to hide from my dad almost every day. I felt hate for my dad for all the experiences for ten years. After another ten years and self-development, I realised that this soul had sacrificed his life for the sake of others so that all the souls in his circle have all the experiences meant for them. I realised how much this soul must have loved all of us to sacrifice so much for the sake of our experiences. I went through a lot of realisations before I understood that I had nothing to forgive my dad for. I have to apologise to him for not being able to understand why all this is happening—for my own sake because the experiences I have had have made me a woman with strong values. Thanks to the lessons I have learned, I can build meaningful relationships. Thanks to my dad, I have a life and a choice of how to live. I apologised to my dad for judging him; I apologised for not seeing his own pain; I apologised for not understanding how his mother had hurt him; I apologised for not understanding his love language because, in spite of everything, he only loved the way he knew how to love. A person who has not experienced love cannot give what he has not known or experienced. I apologised...

My own journey to re-establishing my relationship with my dad took place through my awakener and coach, Milda Sabiene. Milda has lived through family and business crises herself. She has been married for more than 25 years and has two daughters and a granddaughter. Milda is in love with life and travel.

She is an internationally renowned holistic coach and business psychologist, a co-author of two international bestsellers. Milda successfully organises experiential trips for women around the world. I remember the first time I saw her live—I felt her energy, which is hard to describe but easily felt. She can empathize very well with each person, feel their problems, and find answers that a person himself didn't think to be looking for. Milda works in the same direction with entrepreneurs, helping them to refine and grow. I admire her phenomenal ability to connect matter with spirit.

Milda is the kind of person who will tell you exactly how it is, without wrapping things in cotton wool. I asked my teacher, who is an expert in this field, directly about her relationship with her dad and how it relates to money. Directly to you.

MILDA GIFTS YOU HER INSIGHTS INTO THE RELATIONSHIP WITH DAD AND ITS RELATION TO MONEY:

You may be wondering - "How does the amount of money I earn/ get or my relationship with money relate to my relationship with my dad? After all, they are completely different things!"

The world is not about individual things or events. Everything in the world is related, it's just a question of whether we are able to see and understand it. But whether or not we see the connections, the laws of the Universe apply to us all.

PARENTS are the two main people in our lives. Because we were born when they connected. And in their connection, two families were connected in us.

Through our relationship with our parents, we build a relationship with our family and its resources/energy. It's not just about talents, character traits, illnesses, or DNA, but also about money and abundance.

Not only our resources but also our blocks, fears, prohibitions, and losses lie in our family.

To live the life of our dreams, to enjoy success, relationships, recognition, abundance, career, finances, creativity, and fulfilment, we need a relationship with both mum and dad. We walk through life limping because of having a negative relationship with one of our parents, full of anger, hatred, resentment, and ignorance.

The relationship with dad is our key to abundance and fullness of life.

Through the masculine energy we receive from dad, we get the ability to set and achieve goals, the determination and courage to act, and the ability to earn big money. This is the power of our inner man. And it is the quality of this inner strength that determines our relationship with dad.

Our relationship with dad also determines how well we know how to draw boundaries and say "NO," how we allow ourselves to be displeasing to others with no fear while remaining true to ourselves, and how we dare not to judge someone else's expectations because we are not afraid of being rejected.

If you do not accept your dad, if you deny him, or preach to him because he is not good enough, etc., you don't accept men because they are not worthy. There is no respect and no authority. And this is also reflected in your relationship with money. You can make a lot of money, but you can also squander it. You can live a rich life, but there will be an endless feeling of emptiness inside, and you will try in every way to fill it. This is usually through addictions—intoxicants, drugs, casinos, or the constant desire to be the best (competition and comparison with others) so that someone else appreciates and sees you.

Consciously or unconsciously, when we deny dad, we deny ourselves! We are cutting the branch on which we sit and, like children, we are angry that life is not going well or not going the way we want it to.

It doesn't matter whether you grew up with your dad, how much you knew him, or how long he was in your life. One thing is true—without your dad's seed, you would not be here today!

Until you learn to see and accept the infinite resource in your parents, your life will be like a battlefield. It is impossible to accept your parents if you do not feel grateful to them for the life you have received through them.

How do you know if you accept your parents? If you:

• preach to your parents (becoming a parent to your parents),

• interfere in their lives,

• regulate and teach them what to do,

• have no respect for your parents' lives, paths, and choices,

• help your parents out of guilt,

• rescue your parents from their lives,

• reproach them,

• blame them for your life and childhood,

• demand love, recognition, and attention from your parents, this means you are still stuck in your childhood and are not yet able to accept or be grateful.

And it's your choice whether you continue to wallow in the same situations or decide to grow up and deal with your life and your relationship with your mum and dad as adults.

YIN AND YANG

15

YIN AND YANG

L ife is all about balance: night is followed by day, hours of sadness are followed by light and joy, and work is followed by rest. There is also a balance of masculine and feminine energies in human relationships—Yin and Yang. In this chapter, I will talk about the masculine and feminine ways of making money and the importance of the balance of feminine and masculine energies for abundance and prosperity. I will also look at why the feminist movement goes against women's nature and how to find a natural way to make money.

Each person is made up of half masculine and half feminine energy. This comes from nature—men are hunters and conquerors, and women are fosterers of cosiness and warmth and influential partners and creators. When one energy takes over a part of the other—when women shift to the masculine energy or vice versa—internal conflicts begin: women fight and picket while men sit on the couch, afraid to move. When money energy is out of balance, financial problems arise, often leading to emotional outbursts or apathy. Relationships are then dominated by competition, control, aggression, abuse, victim position, apathy, and avoidance. Therefore, it is important to respect our own nature and feel inwardly the paths that lead to prosperity and natural abundance.

WOMAN'S MONEY

A woman attracts and earns money through intuition, generosity, creativity, cooperation, care, and gratitude. Feminine energy relates to the being and is expressed through emotions. *It is inwardly focused, so the feminine energy manifests the acceptance/receiving—inwards, inside, at home, inside the home.* I am not talking here about demanding from the husband because when you demand, you go through a negative intention, you are in low vibrations. A woman who wants to receive from her husband must first give. It is a wonderful Yin-Yang bargain, where a woman combines all the supportive and motivating qualities of a man, and a man maximises his potential and gives back to a woman by showing attention, care, building up family capital, and sharing finances. Yes, a woman's money can come through her husband, and they can enjoy life and prosperity together.

It is welcome and rewarding when a woman earns money through an activity she loves. She does what she likes, and money comes as a result. A woman can live in abundance by fulfilling herself and giving value to others. In the activities she loves, she opens herself up to creativity, pools all her talents, shares her knowledge, works at her own pace, and attracts the natural money energy. If a woman's spouse earns a good income and provides for the family, she can spend her money on pleasure, self-education, and improving her health—she does not have to compete with her husband.

We have to bear in mind the fact that if a woman's central planet is Mars, she is destined to build a business and to lead and make money through her masculine energy. And everything is fine with that. This woman simply has to remember to leave Mars at work and return home to her husband with a softer, feminine energy. The key is to maintain the balance. Or otherwise, she will end up in ongoing competition. Being in Mars, a woman can reveal her feminine side through other energetics, i.e., through eight feminine archetypes. We also engage in these practices at the White Growth Studio. By looking into and refining the strengths, weaknesses, and empowerment of her archetypes, a woman becomes the master of her life and is in full flow through all eight archetypes. A woman flows in, flowing in its activities, relationships, and in her whole being.

FEMINISM

Femina is Latin for "woman". Feminism is a women's movement. In my opinion, nowadays, feminism has gone beyond all boundaries of decency and no longer reflects the true purpose of the movement. At some point, things went too far, and a feminist woman became a warrior princess, forgetting her nature and the givens of nature. Feminism is now about humiliating men and their nature. Total disrespect for feminine nature. Where are you, woman, where are you going, what winds are you fighting? As I said, the feminine nature is to be in a flow, in harmony, and in concord. A woman is the one who accepts, while feminism is about demanding, about putting the female Ego above men. It turns out that women use masculine energy (war, struggle, victory) to fight for their rights. If women are going into feminism, they should do it through their feminine energy—then they won't have to struggle to survive. If they stand in the flowing energy, they will get money more naturally and easily.

MAN'S MONEY

A man attracts and earns money through logic, self-confidence, focus, strength, objectivity, clarity, and excitement in the pursuit of his goals. Masculine energy is about getting things done and is expressed through rationality. *It is outwardly focused and manifests giving, provision, security.* Men go to war, conquer the business world, and earn money through their achievements. It is normal for them to face difficulties and overcome them to get the end result. Of course, a man takes his catch home—shows it to his woman, and is appreciated/unappreciated. It is important to note the strong influence of women as partners on a man's achievements and the money he earns. When a woman is able to give her partner the essentials, she unlocks his enormous potential. A man needs the following from a woman to be fulfilled, to achieve his goals, and to make money:

• unconditional respect

• support and encouragement

• gratitude

Unconditional respect for a man's choices means allowing him to learn from his mistakes. In this way, he enters the masculine energy. A woman does not have to be a mother: explaining everything, telling how to do things, how to dress, when and where to go, and what to say. Men are good at handling everything themselves. It is enough for a woman to respect his decision and to *support* him when he makes a mistake, to guide him on a different path, and *encourage him* to search for a solution. A man needs encouragement and support, and another mistake women make is comparing their husbands, directly or indirectly, to other men—more successful, more generous, etc. A man's potential is fulfilled when he knows that he is the only one to his partner and the only one she needs, otherwise, why would he bring home the catch? He is generous when he feels appreciated, so expressing *gratitude* motivates him to act. We must understand that no one is obliged to do anything. So when a man brings flowers, makes the bed, puts things away, or washes his plate, notice and thank him for that. When people are in relationships, they somehow get used to taking things for granted—small favours, hugs, household chores, etc. It is worth remembering how each act was celebrated at the beginning of the relationship. It is useful for partners to develop this quality in future relationships. Thanking more often, even for the smallest things. When talking and solving problems, it is advisable to refrain from blaming, demanding, blackmailing and manipulating, being open and honest, talking exclusively about yourself, your feelings and experiences, and finding the answers to the questions that concern you. Women, in particular, are able to find the right time for a conversation, approach through flexibility and gentleness, and create a safe environment to talk. Then men definitely hear them!

I will share with you my own experience. I lived with one man for eight years. We competed with each other, as both of ours central planets were Mars. As I had forgotten entirely my feminine nature back then, my verses, and my power through flexibility, we used to fight constantly, debate, and argue in our relationship—tension over money and arguing about who is smarter. I gave my man support through the mother's archetype. And when a woman treats a man like a mother treats her child, there is no room for a meaningful relationship. Men simply don't see such women. The same applies when a man treats his woman in an overprotective way, like a father. My relationship failed for many reasons, and my non-feminine way of acting did not help to solve problems. I am currently in a relationship with my soul twin. Our journey is completely different. Yes, I met my husband after my inner transformation, after becoming the kind of woman I have admired all my life. My husband now gets my support and sometimes a retreat when I see that I need to step back from his affairs and let him manage them as he sees fit. I don't tell him how and what to do (I feel it could be better for him). Instead, I point, ask, keep quiet, smile, listen when he speaks, and admire—I come through the archetype of Aphrodite or the Muse. When I met my husband, he was already successful, earning a five-figure sum, but he wanted to jump two more steps in his career. I was able to approach him through my feminine nature, to support him in the way he needed, and today my husband has achieved his dream position, generating several times more income.

When a woman and a man act according to their nature, the balance of Yin and Yang creates true prosperity—partners complement each other, exchanging energies. When a woman and a man are involved in business and both act according to their nature, they form a great tandem: the woman fills the man through communion, direction, support, flexibility, listening, and respect for his decisions, and the man empowers all his talents and skills, and gets the job done—he achieves his goal. Yin and Yang compatibility in business and in relationships is the closest and most successful path to abundance and to a harmonious life, of course.

MONEY IN THE FAMILY

16

FAMILY MONEY

A family is a group of people living together, committed to each other, in close relationships, and sharing a common household, with or without children, and possibly with pets. A family is a responsible partnership that needs to get its financial affairs in order. In the chapter "Family Money", I will discuss how people living together manage their money, how to go for abundance with the right direction of the natural energy and not block the financial energy of the partner, how a happy/unhappy woman influences her husband's financial achievements and the powerful exchanges that take place in harmonious relationships.

What is important to know about money in a family?

1. It is important for both a woman and a man to have their own money, their own separate bank accounts.

Remember that men and women have different financial energy flows. Men create harmonious relationships by focusing their financial energy on taking action, on achieving a goal. Women work by intuition.

Women are interested in earning money through self-fulfilment, and the process and sharing are just as important as a result. Therefore, a *family cannot have a joint account where both partners receive their salary.* Having one joint account makes the flow of money vulnerable on an energetic level because a man and a woman have separate money energies and need a separate source through which their money comes. Moreover, each person has personal motives, blocks, karmic relationships with money, and alignment of the planets, so two energetically disparate flows cannot be blended into one. A man and a woman must have separate bank accounts and separate money.

2. A woman can (and should) not know how much money her husband earns. Unless the husband himself tells her that.

Men in particular need to have money of their own, which women don't know about, and which they can spend where they want to and how they want. This is a significant intention to maintain male energy. A woman should stay out of her husband's finances, his wallet, and masculine control energy. A woman can guide a man. To take care of her family, she simply tells her husband that she needs to pay taxes or their children's extracurricular activities, and her partner figures out how to give her the required amount. When a man wants to provide money for his wife's personal expenses, he decides on the amount himself. There is no need to make demands of a man—a simple, natural conversation at the right time produces results and builds trust.

3. The allocation of costs for housing, living expenses, children, and leisure is a matter of mutual agreement between the partners.

There are families where more of the money flows through a man—he provides for the family, and a woman doesn't have to work her head off to earn money—she can do what she likes or help her husband in his business. It is then important for the woman to support her husband, to guide and encourage him, and to inspire him to take on big projects—in response, the man shares his achievements, his abundance, and there is an energy and material exchange taking place. When a woman is happy, provided for, in her own flow, and secure, she gives her energy to her man and intuitively encourages him to act. When a woman is unhappy, she has a negative impact not only on her own financial situation but also on that of her family. Her energy level is blocked, and her husband is often prevented from achieving his goals, growing his business, and supporting his family. If both partners work and earn well, they decide how to share their family's common expenses. In general, it is important to agree within a family how the money will be divided and who will pay for what to avoid disputes. From time to time, finances can be redistributed according to the money coming into the family.

4. A joint bank account is a secondary account where partners' money is transferred for joint family expenses.

It is advisable to open a joint family account where money agreed by both partners is deposited every month to be allocated to various expenses: utility bills, rent or loan payments, holidays, investments, etc. This is joint family money, spent as agreed.

 Here are some practices that help to put family finances in order:

• Energy practices to unblock money energy.

• Creative practice for establishing a family bond and blessing.

• Removal of sexual imprints.

• Getting relationships with parents in order.

• Working personally on yourself and your natural talents.

I apply all these practices in the White Growth Studio during targeted sessions.

Every family has its own methods of managing its finances. It is important not to violate the fundamental laws of abundance and let each family member's money energy flow in its own way. This also applies to children when they start receiving their first money. First, children see their parents as role models at the financial level and often copy their parents. Secondly, children need to be taught financial literacy with advice rather than blind control. When you take responsibility, when you get some experience, you learn the lessons of life, including financial management.

In a family, being in the natural flow—masculine or feminine, having a supportive partner, encouragement (especially for men!)—have a big impact on financial success. In order to receive full feedback from her husband, a woman must give to him:

• Gratitude

• Support

• Unconditional respect

• Meet his sexual needs

Family harmony and balance are promoted by the relinquishing of control and mutual agreement on common expenses. At the same time, the separation of sources of financial income is the first prerequisite for money to come into the family easier.

SEXUAL IMPRINTS

SEXUAL IMPRINTS

This law is exclusively meant for women because sexual imprints are energetic traces that remain in a woman after every sexual encounter with her partner. A woman establishes an energetic connection with every man with whom she has sex. You may wonder: "What does this have to do with money?"

Sexual energy is strongly related to money energy. As I have already mentioned, the energy of money is very powerful, and most people are simply unable to deal with it and accept it. People who win huge sums of money in lotteries are often energetically unprepared to accept large amounts of money, so they waste it. This is not just about a lack of financial literacy, but it's an energetic unpreparedness to accept. Entrepreneurs find themselves in similar situations - when they get more profit, they panic and lose direction. I have seen many such cases. My clients say: "I had big money come in, and I lost it, I earned again, and I lost it again, I don't understand what's going on, how do I deal with that?" or "Everything seems to be in place, everything is supposed to be moving forward, but it's not—I am stuck." We then do one energetic practice that helps us to determine whether, on an energetic level, the person is ready to accept the flow of money. There are cases when a client is only prepared to earn a living, and no more, or his energy is directed to work for someone else, but he tries to do business and earn from it. Money is blocked and does not reach him. But after a person practices clearing energy blocks, money starts flowing. An energetically prepared person can accept money.

Money energy is born in the second chakra, which is also home to sexual and creative energy. This means that sexual energy is also strong —creating or destroying, depending on sexual lifestyle, choice of partners, stability, etc., and this is especially true for women.

What is a modern woman like? Often she is rushing, overworked, dissatisfied with everything, frustrated with her life, and lacking self-fulfilment. There are large outflows of energy, which exhaust her. This is because the woman still has energetic ties with her former partners. Her life is ruined by the sexual imprints that remain:

• either after the many men who have entered her;

• or after a difficult relationship with one partner.

Any emotional or sexual relationships connect a woman to a man for seven years. All this time, a woman, as a giver, is a "feeder" for these men. A part of her energy is feeding a man every day, so she may feel involuntarily tired, exhausted as if she was drunk, guilty, resentful, frustrated, angry, and unable to experience a sense of intimacy. She carries these imprints within her and even transmits her bad emotions, remaining resentments, reproaches, etc., to the man she currently lives with. In communication with her current partner, she sometimes reacts and does not understand her own reaction triggered by her sexual imprints—the energetic connection with her former partners. It hurts the woman's emotional state, drains her energy, and impairs her partnership relationships. It has been observed that a woman who wears sexual imprints also blocks her husband's ability to earn money.

I want to share my experience. I have already mentioned that I lived in a difficult karmic relationship for eight years. My partner and I had never got on well in our personal life. Our divorce also lasted for a year. I only managed to break the last energetic umbilical cord after the practice of removing sexual imprints. I got an initiation from my teacher and did the practice to the end. Then my partner and I started to hear each other (which hadn't been the case for all those eight years), and we went into a conscious divorce. Half a year after doing this practice, I met my soul twin, which is a wonderful breakthrough in my relationship, and I owe it to the practice of removing sexual imprints. My example is ending a toxic relationship with one partner and clearing the energies. But before this partner, my sex life was out of control and loose. And casual sex had a big impact on my relationship with money. There are many such women who do not shy away from casual sex and indulge without choosing who to share their sexual energy with, sacrificing their financial stability, their potential, and their ability to flourish in natural abundance. When a woman allows any man who wants to feed on her energy into her lotus, energetic, destructive processes take place. A woman is not filled with anger, aggression, and pain of another. This is how she collects from each man a piece of who he is and what he feels. Men also transmit other women's reproaches, frustrations, and emotions via their phallus. Because by nature, the male organ is outward-facing, while a woman's genitals are inward-facing, going inwards. Everything that goes inside a woman stays there for seven years! *For seven years, a woman carries an energetic connection with every man she has slept with.* For seven years, a woman gives away her energy to her former partners as if through silver threads that flow out of her body. I have seen many cases of what is called the Telegony Effect, where, say, a woman has been in a relationship with one man for two years, then starts another relationship, then has a child a year later. The newborn child carries the character traits of her ex. It sounds frightening, but a woman can give birth to a baby that is not her husband's (although the original seed is her current husband's, but the energetics, sometimes even physical similarities, are those of her former partner). The energetic connection left in a woman is passed on to the nascent life. This is how the Telegony Effect works. Thus it is essential to remove sexual imprints so that women can function normally—to build a fulfilling relationship with a partner, to extend kinship, and to accept and manage the natural flow of money.

Since sexual energy is money energy, a woman who gives herself away to men:

• either is always out of money;

• or can't earn it;

• or money slips out of her hands - is spent without her even knowing how much money she has or how much she earns;

• or she entrusts her business to her husband because she doubts her ability to manage her personal finances.

In reality, women have enormous potential to earn and manage money, but they have given themselves over to men. A woman has an energetic connection with all her partners and does not understand why she gravitates towards men and trusts only them. Her energy has already been distributed, so subconsciously she attracts a man to manage her business money.

A woman who sleeps around, who has a strong desire, a passion for having sex—as she wants it all the time—has crossed over into the field of masculine energy. She should be concerned about and look for ways to unleash her inner feminine energy to channel her sexual energy into creativity, abandoning casual, frequent, and emotionally unstable sexual relationships. Sexual energy is a creative energy that should be empowered in activities, work, hobbies, rendering great results: self-fulfilment and abundance.

For a woman to have a natural flow of money and a good relationship with money, she must first have pure sexual energy:

• either have no casual relationships with men,

• or clear out all the sexual relationships and negative energy that have been present for seven years.

Both women and men want to build harmonious relationships, to start with a clean slate. Men want to marry women who are energetically clean, and women want to marry men who are reliable and free from the toxic shadow of their relationships. Imprint removal practices help to clear sexual energy and to start life with a clean slate.

Every sexual act, every sexual encounter, leaves threads in a woman through which her energy outflows. The practice of removing sexual imprints releases the energy of abundance, cleanses women of their attachments, and removes emotional baggage. The flow of removing energetic traces of former partners destroys energetic imprints left by them in the physical and emotional body matrix of women.

Dear women, love your lotus, learn to hold back. If you have had many partners in the last seven years, do the practice of removing sexual imprints. Having done it, you will open the gateway to the flow of money energy for yourself, your husband, and your family.

ANCESTOR BLESSING

18

ANCESTRAL BLESSING

I have already talked about a person's karma in the chapter on "Astrology and Karma," focusing on the person's money karma from past lives and how he can improve the karmic relationship with money by living honestly in the present life. In this chapter, I will talk about money karma of kin that a person is born with and how it influences life on a financial level, in creating personal happiness, and how the kin karma can be recoded/reprogrammed through practices.

The human soul chooses to be born in a particular family, chooses the parents, the environment, the childhood experiences, chooses to be born in a particular kin, and therefore brings with him the karma of that kin and the unresolved issues, as well as the karma of the kin's money. Here I would like to note that the *money karma of kin is directly related to the money energy of a person.* Ancestral money karma flows through karmic channels from the past to the future over seven generations, creating a flow from the source of the kin itself. If someone in the family has not followed the laws of karma, then this source becomes scarce and polluted, passing on everything that has accumulated to future generations. If you have relatives who used to steal or cheat, chances are that:

• a person will be prone to theft and cheating himself;

• or that person will be cheated by others—ripped off, swindled out of money, etc.;

• or both.

The law of kin's money karma works on a cause-and-effect basis, through seven generations of the kin counting from the parents. Thus, a person's financial success is influenced by the lifestyle of as many as 128 ancestors (parents - grandparents - grandparents' parents - great-grandparents' parents, etc.). It looks impressive but also hopeless—what should I do? How can I attract abundance if I had wicked ancestors, especially in the immediate generations? How can I know what they were like, given that these are seven generations, a family tree going back 150-200 years? Did my ancestors steal, or, just the opposite, support others financially; did they cheat or were they honest; were they rich or poor, hating the rich, in a lot of debt? There are many questions, even having analysed one's family tree well. Of course, feats of our ancestors and stories about them can be exaggerated in order to exalt them. One thing is clear—kin karma is very powerful.

The word "karma" is understood as destiny, fate. Ancient Eastern sages used to define karma as an action: a thought—a word—an action. This proves that people have known about the existence of karma since time immemorial. Today, judging a bad deed, people say: "You won't get far with such karma," or having done something good: "I got karma points, I cleared my karma." As if understanding that actions determine the future. But still, going back to jealousy, anger, boastfulness, violence (physical and psychological), wanton waste, or fraud. All these experiences cause aggression in the human soul, taking a person to low vibrations and draining his energy. They also affect the flow of money energy. Money flows, like any other form of energy, should flow freely through a person's space without stagnation. But now, this energy has a thick, jelly-like viscous state. This leads to various crises in people's lives, including financial losses. So what has the biggest influence on people's happiness? Past and present. What is equally important? The future of humanity, and the well-being of future generations in particular. A person's past and present determine his future. Everything is simple: the principle of cause and effect, or *karma*.

People underestimate their past and live in the present. The present is the direct result of the deeds of a person and his seven generations. Individual episodes from a person's past life flash in dreams but often go unrecognised. Thus, to prevent kin's money karma from destroying one's life and to attract natural abundance, kin's money energy can be cleansed and restored.

Restoring the energy of your kin's money is about saving yourself and future generations. It is about reuniting with our ancestors and their blessing. We also do karma cleansing of the money of our kin at the White Growth Studio. There are several effective practices that both men and women can do:

• A money tree for seven generations.

• Restoring kin's money energy.

The practices go back seven generations and cleanse money karmas of all generations, reprogramming the codes each ancestor brings with them at birth and creates in life. This is how the blessing of our ancestors is obtained. It's a big job that relaxes, takes away blocks, and gives a clean slate to start from.

Let's say a woman is, or decides to be, the guardian of her family's/kin's money energy. All she has to do is to perform practices of cleansing of money energy of her kin—reprogramming her own money energy and money energy of her future generations. She can do the same with her husband's kin's money karma—to cleanse the money energy of her husband and his future generations. Then children who do not have the programmed family money codes—on their mother's and father's side, from seven generations of the kin—will be born to this family. It is, therefore, worth taking care of yourself, your children, and your grandchildren by removing karmic blocks to money, releasing the financial energy of current and future relatives, and moving towards abundance.

To sum up, everything is important: my own way of life and the foundation created by past generations - the energy field of money. The most important thing is to seek a positive relationship with your ancestors, to understand them, and to thank them—they were probably doing the best they knew and could do. Let go of grievances and thank. Because you are here and you can change it all—do money energy cleansing practices, let go of poverty and scarcity thinking, be honest with yourself and those around you, take your life to a higher level, raise vibrational frequencies that will attract opportunities and abundance, and thank, again and again. To create favourable karmic conditions for the future life on earth for Yourself and your children. After all, money energy is the divine flow of money.

19

GOLD

You may be wondering why there is yet another chapter called "Gold". Gold is not a law but rather a principle of money attraction that I learned from the entrepreneur, writer, and investment expert Robert Kiyosaki. No, I don't know him personally yet. But I have read all of Kiyosaki's books, and I want to share how investing in gold can attract money and increase income.

Mr. Kiyosaki has had a profound impact on my life, changing the way I think about money and, in turn, changing my financial life. In fact, I changed it myself because I followed a lot of Kiyosaki's advice and took the initiative. As I have previously mentioned, knowledge is not enough, you have to take action, and his books inspired me to take actual steps. This is the author whose ideas hooked me, and I started my own journey of learning about the world of money. There was an insatiable appetite for knowledge and motivation to take action myself and build a promising life. Rich Dad, Poor Dad, was the gateway to learning about the laws of money energy and putting them into practice successfully. The phase leading up to this book was not completely empty—I was always looking for information about earning potential, about the flow of money energy—but it dots the i's, and tangible progress in my life began.

WHY GOLD?

Gold is the money of the gods. It is a luxury metal that people adorn themselves with and invest in as a valuable investment. Since ancient times, people have been overwhelmed by *a gold rush*. Travellers and gold seekers have endlessly searched for *veins of gold* on different continents. Wars have been fought over areas where gold is mined. The *Golden Age* is described in the dictionary of idioms as a happy period, a carefree life, a time when a nation's art, science, and history flourished. How often do we look for the *golden middle* in life—the harmonious line between excess and deficiency? And a good idea, a solution, a visionary thought is called a *golden thought*. *Gold is associated with wealth, value, and good life in people's minds.* Mr. Kiyosaki himself says: "The global market for gold and silver transcends borders, politics, religion and race. A person may not like someone else's religion, but he will accept his gold."

The "gold" principle, which Kiyosaki also uses, reflects a simple law of attraction: gold attracts money. It works for me, too, and has been tested many times. However, I would like to note that the Gold Principle does not work for everyone.

How does the Gold principle work?

I buy gold with the intention of investing and increasing my income by the amount which I used to buy gold. Let's say I want to increase my earnings by £200 in a few months. I buy £200 worth of gold and put it away safely. The important thing is to forget that gold. Then it does its work, and a few months later, my income increases by £200. I then repeat the action to reinforce the law of attraction. I buy £200 worth of gold again and put it in a safe place without thinking about it. If I keep thinking: "I bought gold, where is my increased income? When will I get rich? Why doesn't the principle work?" etc., then the principle will not work. It is necessary to deal with your stream of thoughts and leave the gold alone. The Gold Rule also does not work for people who do it with the intent of greed—when the intent is to get rich rather than to make money from the idea, the principle "money for money's sake" prevails

Another thing is that an investment in gold in anticipation of the attraction of money must be well-measured. Let's say I bought gold for £200 a few times, and the third time I decided to spend £1,000 on it. I probably don't believe I can attract that kind of money myself, and thus I move into the "greed" intent. The logical progression disappears, and the principle no longer works. And if you do it right—by gradually increasing the amounts, letting your gold rest, controlling your thoughts, and, of course, working efficiently—the result may come.

I wish everyone to find the golden middle when investing in gold. May golden thoughts visit you in your work. Go into abundance at your own pace, true to yourself, and committed to your mission. Let consistency be the key to the outcome full of good.

THE END

First of all, I want to thank you for making this book reach you, and if you are reading this line, this means you also got to know the 18 Money Energy Laws. I am very happy to share my knowledge, and I believe you will find it useful. Finally, here are ten key steps to attract wealth that anyone can take without any initial capital.

1. *Create such an environment at home where everything makes you happy. Take a look around your house to see what things are there. If you find something you haven't even noticed for a long time, get rid of it. Leave ONLY those things at home which you notice and that make you feel good when you look at them.*

2. *Allow yourself to dream in detail about what you really want, why you want it, and what exactly you will do to make it happen.*

3. *Transform limiting beliefs about money into a positive. This practice can be done in writing.*

4. *When you spend money, spend it with plea-sure. Avoid feelings of guilt and shame.*

5. Avoid debt. If you have any, pay them back wisely or turn debt into good debt.

6. Change the intention from "how to earn money to survive" to "how to fulfil yourself and add value for others." The longer you think about it, the sooner your thoughts will take a physical form.

7. Meditate and let yourself feel worthy of living well and comfortably.

8. For any dream, intention, or manifestation to come true, remember— you have to do something. Only continuous growth and continuous action will produce real results. Combine these powers with visualisations.

9. Abundance comes not only in the form of paper or electronic money but also in the form of free services, gratitude, and gifts. ACCEPT it, and be sure to thank.

10. Spend money. Money is energy and cannot stand still.

It's easier to be happy when you live in abundance. Happiness is what I can do with the money I have. I am sure that everyone has noble goals:

• save the world from global warming

• build an animal shelter

• donate money to families in need

• support sick children

• help the elderly

• feed the hungry

• contribute to eliminating food insecurity around the world, etc.

What can a person do having no money? That's right, nothing. We should not fall into spirituality and consciousness with extremes because spirituality is just another ego. After all, we have a physical body, thus we came here to also experience materiality and earthly life. If you learn to live spiritually, you will learn to be a human being. Socialize with others, share your experiences and knowledge, learn how to build a family, be a parent, a friend, establish a business, or build a community. Learn to learn. Know that there is no single truth. Truth is the Source (God) And the Source is different. It is everything and nothing. Become shapeless like water. Water adapts to each container it is poured into. Learn with a childlike curiosity. Remember to rejoice at least three times every day. Joy raises vibrations. Laughter raises vibrations. And everything happens smoother and more pleasant in high vibrations. Money energy walks gracefully and abundantly in high vibrations. Be rich before you earn big money. I wish you happiness and plenitude.

ABOUT THE AUTHOR

VALENTINA WHITE

Valentina White is a Transformation Coach currently leading individuals to complete life satisfaction and abundance. In 10 years' of running her finance firm, she has developed a unique teaching of 18 Money Energy Laws and has become a Master of Money Energy. She is a successful entrepreneur, nominated as Businesswoman and CFO of 2021.

Her ability to convert fears into inspiration saved countless businesses from pandemic failures and helped restructure several companies from one trade to another.

Her mission is to share knowledge, inspire and heal individual money flow through awakening the natural abundance. Her unique coaching style and programmes allow her clients to achieve complete satisfaction in life and business.

Find out more: https://whitegrowth.studio/

Printed in Great Britain
by Amazon